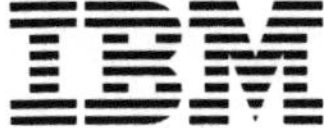

International Technical Support Organization

Planning for the Installation and Rollout of WebSphere Studio Application Monitor 3.1

April 2005

SG24-7072-00

Note: Before using this information and the product it supports, read the information in “Notices” on page vii.

First Edition (April 2005)

This edition applies to Version 3, Release 1, Modification 0 of WebSphere Studio Application Monitor for Multiplatforms (product number 5724-K79).

© Copyright International Business Machines Corporation 2005. All rights reserved.
Note to U.S. Government Users Restricted Rights -- Use, duplication or disclosure restricted by GSA ADP Schedule Contract with IBM Corp.

Contents

© Copyright IBM Corp. 2005. All rights reserved.

Notices

This information was developed for products and services offered in the U.S.A.

IBM may not offer the products, services, or features discussed in this document in other countries. Consult your local IBM representative for information on the products and services currently available in your area. Any reference to an IBM product, program, or service is not intended to state or imply that only that IBM product, program, or service may be used. Any functionally equivalent product, program, or service that does not infringe any IBM intellectual property right may be used instead. However, it is the user's responsibility to evaluate and verify the operation of any non-IBM product, program, or service.

IBM may have patents or pending patent applications covering subject matter described in this document. The furnishing of this document does not give you any license to these patents. You can send license inquiries, in writing, to:
IBM Director of Licensing, IBM Corporation, North Castle Drive Armonk, NY 10504-1785 U.S.A.

The following paragraph does not apply to the United Kingdom or any other country where such provisions are inconsistent with local law: INTERNATIONAL BUSINESS MACHINES CORPORATION PROVIDES THIS PUBLICATION "AS IS" WITHOUT WARRANTY OF ANY KIND, EITHER EXPRESS OR IMPLIED, INCLUDING, BUT NOT LIMITED TO, THE IMPLIED WARRANTIES OF NON-INFRINGEMENT, MERCHANTABILITY OR FITNESS FOR A PARTICULAR PURPOSE. Some states do not allow disclaimer of express or implied warranties in certain transactions, therefore, this statement may not apply to you.

This information could include technical inaccuracies or typographical errors. Changes are periodically made to the information herein; these changes will be incorporated in new editions of the publication. IBM may make improvements and/or changes in the product(s) and/or the program(s) described in this publication at any time without notice.

Any references in this information to non-IBM Web sites are provided for convenience only and do not in any manner serve as an endorsement of those Web sites. The materials at those Web sites are not part of the materials for this IBM product and use of those Web sites is at your own risk.

IBM may use or distribute any of the information you supply in any way it believes appropriate without incurring any obligation to you.

Information concerning non-IBM products was obtained from the suppliers of those products, their published announcements or other publicly available sources. IBM has not tested those products and cannot confirm the accuracy of performance, compatibility or any other claims related to non-IBM products. Questions on the capabilities of non-IBM products should be addressed to the suppliers of those products.

This information contains examples of data and reports used in daily business operations. To illustrate them as completely as possible, the examples include the names of individuals, companies, brands, and products. All of these names are fictitious and any similarity to the names and addresses used by an actual business enterprise is entirely coincidental.

COPYRIGHT LICENSE:
This information contains sample application programs in source language, which illustrates programming techniques on various operating platforms. You may copy, modify, and distribute these sample programs in any form without payment to IBM, for the purposes of developing, using, marketing or distributing application programs conforming to the application programming interface for the operating platform for which the sample programs are written. These examples have not been thoroughly tested under all conditions. IBM, therefore, cannot guarantee or imply reliability, serviceability, or function of these programs. You may copy, modify, and distribute these sample programs in any form without payment to IBM for the purposes of developing, using, marketing, or distributing application programs conforming to IBM's application programming interfaces.

© Copyright IBM Corp. 2005. All rights reserved.

Trademarks

The following terms are trademarks of the International Business Machines Corporation in the United States, other countries, or both:

AIX 5L™
AIX®
CICS®
DB2®
@server®
Hummingbird®
IBM®
ibm.com®
IMS™
MVS™
Parallel Sysplex®
pSeries®
Quantify®
Redbooks™
Redbooks (logo) ™
RACF®
RMF™
Tivoli®
VTAM®
WebSphere®
z/OS®
zSeries®

The following terms are trademarks of other companies:

WS_FTP is a trademark or registered trademark of Ipswitch, Inc. in the United States, other countries, or both.

SecureCRT is a trademark or registered trademark of VanDyke Software, Inc. in the United States, other countries, or both.

WinZip is a trademark or registered trademark of WinZip Computing, Inc. in the United States, other countries, or both.

Oracle is a trademark or registered trademark of Oracle, Inc. in the United States, other countries, or both.

HP-UX is a trademark or registered trademark of Hewlett Packard, Inc. in the United States, other countries, or both.

SUSE is a trademark or registered trademark of SUSE Linux, Inc. in the United States, other countries, or both.

RedHat is a trademark or registered trademark of RedHat, Inc. in the United States, other countries, or both.

WebLogic is a trademark or registered trademark of BEA Systems, Inc. in the United States, other countries, or both.

Java and all Java-based trademarks and Solaris and logos are trademarks or registered trademarks of Sun Microsystems, Inc. in the United States, other countries, or both.

Windows and the Windows logo are trademarks of Microsoft Corporation in the United States, other countries, or both.

Intel and Intel Inside (logos) are trademarks of Intel Corporation in the United States, other countries, or both.

UNIX is a registered trademark of The Open Group in the United States and other countries.

Linux is a trademark of Linus Torvalds in the United States, other countries, or both.

Other company, product, and service names may be trademarks or service marks of others.

Preface

This IBM® Redbook was written for anyone interested in the installation of WebSphere® Studio Application Monitor (WSAM) for Multiplatforms including performance analysts, WebSphere administrators, and technical management. Our goal is to provide a useful overview and positioning of WSAM, and more importantly an overview of the planning required for a WebSphere Studio Application Monitor installation. We also include hints, tips, and other pragmatic "how-to" information to help you install the product and be productive quickly and easily.

This book is not a substitute for the product manuals themselves. You or other members of your team will still need to read the Installation Guide for current installation instructions, and the User Guide for usage information. However, in this book we point out those areas that customers tend to have questions about regarding installation and configuration, and offer suggestions based on our own experience. We also provide a "first place to look," for information on WSAM installation, with pointers to additional documentation and sources for those areas we cannot cover in depth.

The book covers:

- WSAM overview
- Pre-installation planning
- Care and feeding of WSAM
- WSAM installation rollout planning
- Troubleshooting
- Firewalls and ports

The team that wrote this redbook

This redbook was produced by a team of specialists from around the world working at the International Technical Support Organization, Raleigh Center.

Bina Khimani has been working with WebSphere Studio Application Monitor for two years. She has nine years of experience in the applications development area. She holds a Masters degree in Computer Science. She is an adjacent faculty member at the Golden Gate University, San Francisco and Foothill College, Los Altos, California.

Richard Mackler is a Senior IT Architect in the Tivoli® Application Management Group. Previously with Cyanea Systems, he provided installation and support for z/OS®, WSAM, and WebSphere, direct support for WSAM PoCs and Crit-Sit management. His initial professional employment began at Bell Telephone Laboratories as a developer on Military Projects, a Systems Programmer, and developed performance monitoring tools for the Bell System. Transferring to Pacific Bell, he held positions of Systems Programmer, Performance Management for MVS™ systems, Applications Project Architect, Technical Manager and Manager for Security Systems Implementation. After leaving the Bell System, he held positions as Director of Production Services, AVP Computer Operations, Chief Security Officer for an international Bank and security consultant to Charles Schwab. He holds BS and MS degrees in Computer Science and Mathematics.

© Copyright IBM Corp. 2005. All rights reserved.

Thanks to the following people from IBM for their contributions:

Breet “Chuck” Bangle
Nichole Cargill
Arthur “Dennis” Moore
Arun Biligiri

Joe DeCarlo, Manager of Special Projects at the IBM International Technical Support Organization.

Become a published author

Join us for a two- to six-week residency program! Help write an IBM Redbook dealing with specific products or solutions, while getting hands-on experience with leading-edge technologies. You'll team with IBM technical professionals, Business Partners and/or customers.

Your efforts will help increase product acceptance and customer satisfaction. As a bonus, you'll develop a network of contacts in IBM development labs, and increase your productivity and marketability.

Find out more about the residency program, browse the residency index, and apply online at:

ibm.com/redbooks/residencies.html

Comments welcome

Your comments are important to us!

We want our Redbooks™ to be as helpful as possible. Send us your comments about this or other Redbooks in one of the following ways:

- Use the online **Contact us** review redbook form found at:

  ibm.com/redbooks

- Send your comments in an e-mail to:

  redbook@us.ibm.com

- Mail your comments to:

  IBM Corporation, International Technical Support Organization
  Dept. HZ8 Building 662
  P.O. Box 12195
  Research Triangle Park, NC 27709-2195

1

What is WebSphere Studio Application Monitor?

This chapter offers some very brief descriptions about what is new in WebSphere Studio Application Monitor (WSAM) V3.1. Also, in this chapter we discuss WSAM's architecture and major components, what the three monitoring levels are, their implications for in-flight monitoring and historical workload analyses, and an explanation of terminology and concepts surrounding composite request monitoring.

Also, this chapter covers the WSAM installation process. This is an overview - it is not intended to replace either the chapters in this book with detailed installation instructions and procedures, or the WSAM Installation Guides. The brief description is a overview of directions for installing WSAM.

For detailed installation and operational specifics, see:

- *WebSphere Studio Application Monitor Installation and Customization Guide*, SC31-6312
- *WebSphere Studio Application Monitor CICS Data Collector Product Guide*, SC31-6569
- *WebSphere Studio Application Monitor IMS Data collector Product Guide*, SC31-6789
- *WebSphere Studio Application Monitor Operations Guide*, SC31-6313
- *WebSphere Studio Application Monitor Monitoring Console User's Guide*, SC31-6314
- *WebSphere Studio Application Monitor Messages and Codes*, SC31-6315

The latest WSAM documentation is available at:

`http://www.ibm.com/software/awdtools/studioapplicationmonitor/library/`

© Copyright IBM Corp. 2005. All rights reserved.

1.1 What's new in WSAM V3.1

Version 3.1 of WSAM introduces new features and capabilities that enhance the product's monitoring scope, its usefulness and benefit to systems and applications programmers, and its utility as a measurement tool for management-level and executive decision-making. WSAM V3.1 introduces many new capabilities and features.

1.2 Composite request monitoring

Among these new features is *enhanced composite monitoring*, which tracks distributed requests as they travel through different systems and locations. Types of enhanced composite monitoring include:

- J2EE-CICS monitoring:

  Composite monitoring of J2EE requests and spawned CICS® transactions where data is transported between the servers using middleware products like WebSphere MQ or the CICS Transaction Gateway (CTG).

- J2EE-IMS monitoring:

  Composite monitoring of J2EE requests and spawned IMS™ transactions where data is transported between the servers using middleware products like WebSphere MQ or IMSConnect.

- J2EE to J2EE monitoring:

  Composite monitoring of requests that span multiple JVMs where data is transported between the servers using WebSphere MQ. Other transport methods, like RMI over IIOP, are not supported.

- WebSphere MQ monitoring:

  This feature tracks and correlates requests across J2EE to legacy systems, like CICS or IMS, using WebSphere MQ as the middleware data transport mechanism. WebSphere MQ, then, is regarded by WSAM V3.1 as a middleware product like the CICS Transaction Gateway or IMSConnect. The monitoring of queues, brokers, and other WebSphere MQ components is not supported and WSAM system traps will not work with WebSphere MQ processing.

- WebSphere Business Integrator (WBI) monitoring:

  WSAM V3.1 introduces a new Data Collector, WebSphere Business Integration (WBI) Server, that monitors WBI-based adaptors for traditional back-office applications. The first WBI Data Collector will support JDBC adaptors. Support for other adaptors, like those for SAP, is due in early 2005. The WBI Data Collector component will ship after the initial delivery of WSAM V3.1.

1.2.1 Application analysis features

There are new and improved analytical features built into WSAM V3.1.

- Application sizing:

  Selected transaction sets can be summarized and display aggregated information about nested requests (J2EE API calls) and Java™ method calls. This information assists with application sizing studies, for instance, where applications are examined to determine the exact resource requirements for running workloads.

- Capacity analysis:

  Users can request supply versus demand graphs for selected time periods, projecting how future demands might affect enterprise IT resources. These models are based on existing resource consumptions by workloads, and they can project a workload's future needs based on trends measured over time.

- Scheduled reports:

  Detailed historical performance reports are produced by drawing on the monitoring data stowed in WSAM's repository database. WSAM V3.1 extends this reporting feature by adding more scheduling capabilities and options for the reports inventory.

Note: IBM WSAM V3.1 names for software part numbers can change or can be included in the base product as-is. For example, WebSphere MQ monitoring is not a separate PID, but J2EE-to-CICS monitoring is, and is called "Studio Application Monitor for CICS" or "SAM-CICS" for short.

- Installations:
  - Installation prerequisite checking is scripted for use with all pre-installation planning phases.
  - The automatic installation of distributed nodes within a single vertical JVM cluster is supported. However, cross-box or horizontal clustering is not supported.
  - The Managing Server runtime check is scripted and displays information about the real-time health of a Managing Server. It supplements the Managing Server's self-diagnosis features of WSAM.
- Monitoring enhancements:

  Trap suppression is a new feature that will "auto-snooze" once a trap starts to propagate alerts. This prevents traps from flooding systems with unwanted copies of messages and data/problem reports.

- Visualization Engine (VE) enhancements:
  - Skins allow WSAM's VE color theme to be changed independently of the underlying Java code. There is a new default "positive" or dark text on light background theme.
  - Scalability: The WSAM VE is better at handling large numbers of monitored environments through run-time improvements like paginations for large datasets.
  - Top navigation menus: The top navigation choices are reorganized so that options are located under appropriate headings, and more frequently used features are exposed at the top level. For example, Performance Analysis Reporting (PAR) is moved to the top navigation level instead of being one among many items in the more general Performance Analysis top level tab and options found in WSAM v2 and below.

How WSAM delivers these features is in many ways derived from WSAM's architecture. This Redbook focuses on installing WSAM V3.1. We offer high-level information about WSAM and its components; however, the purpose of this Redbook is to explain how to install WSAM.

Next is a brief overview of WSAM's architecture and equally brief discussions about some of WSAM's monitoring capabilities and features.

1.3 Architecture and design

WSAM is made up of multiple components connected across TCP/IP networks. It has a loosely coupled structure with discrete components, many of which can be started up and brought down independently of one another. This means that the product is very scalable, potentially supporting thousands of networked servers through single or multiple operational points of control. Figure 1-1 illustrates WSAM's topology, identifying the major components and where they reside.

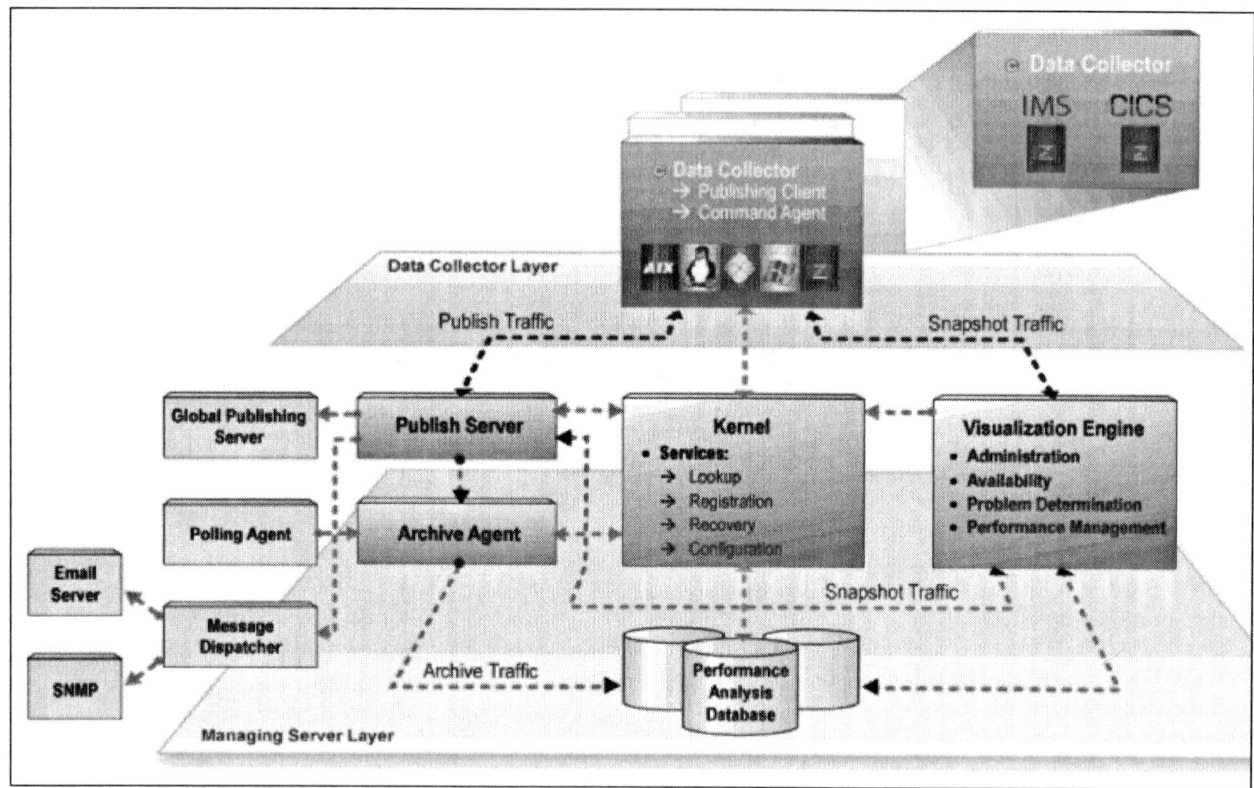

Figure 1-1 WSAM architecture

There are three principal parts to WSAM: A Managing Server which must reside on a distributed platform or on a Linux for zSeries system, distributed data collectors, and z/OS data collectors. The Managing Server houses a relational database like DB2® UDB, an instance of WebSphere Application Server running the WSAM console application, and Java-based overseer components that control the Managing Server itself and the storage of monitoring data. As might be expected, very I/O-intensive operations go on in the Managing Server. Moving these processes to the Managing Server means that they do impact the performance of the monitored servers or their platforms.

The data collectors are built for dexterity and speed. They unleash probes that gather up monitoring data about applications running in J2EE servers or in legacy systems like CICS or IMS. Each Data Collector is written to take advantage of speedy and efficient services available on the host operating system. For example, the z/OS WebSphere Data Collector uses MVS Cross-Memory Services to transport data between address spaces, CSAM and ISAM run their probes and supporting routines in legacy systems under separate TCBs to keep their footprints out of production workload processing. The relationships between the Managing Server and Data Collectors can be illustrated as shown in Figure 1-2 on page 5.

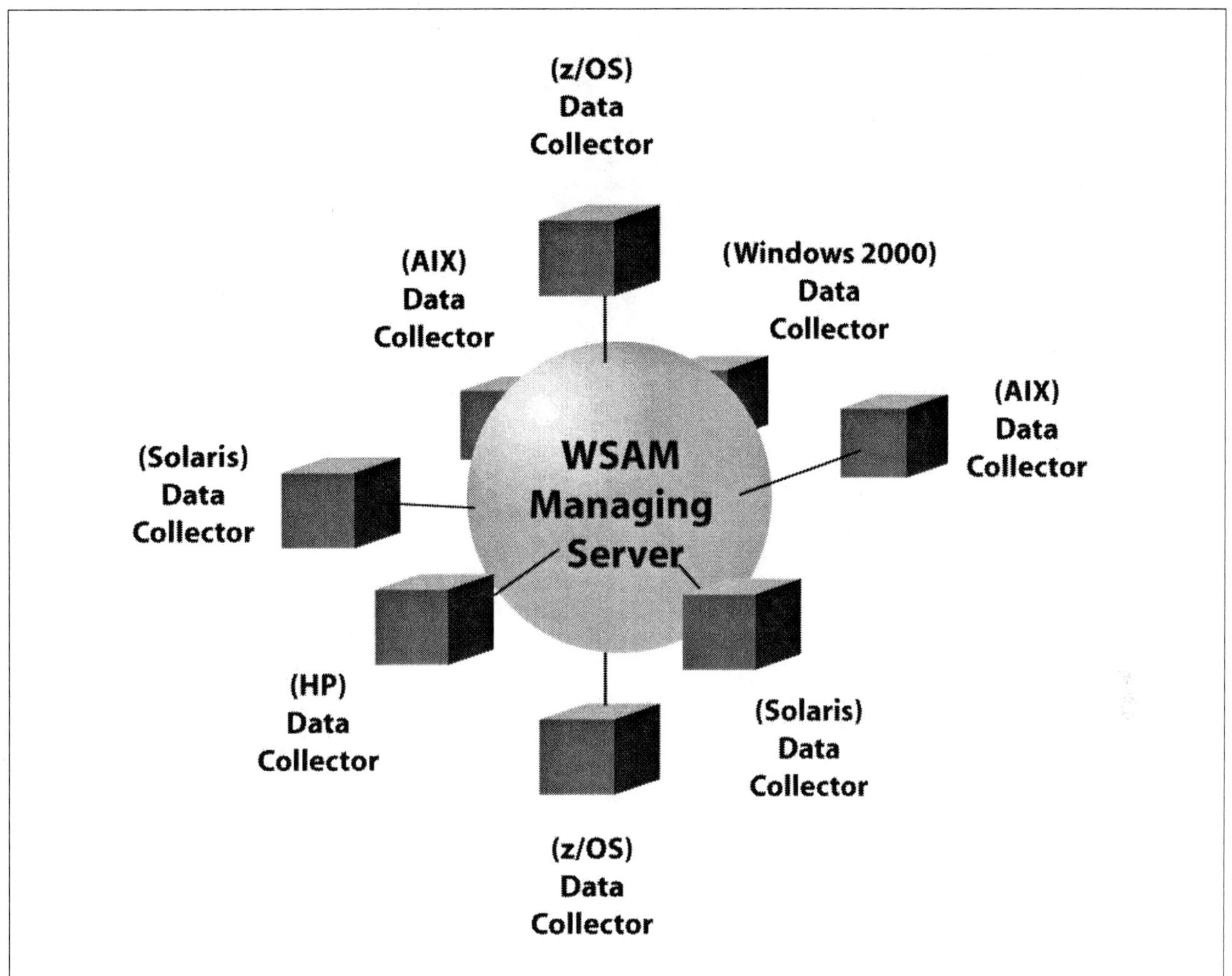

Figure 1-2 WSAM diagram 1

1.3.1 The Managing Server

WSAM's Managing Server (MS) controls and coordinates data collectors (DC) for J2EE or legacy servers that run user applications. Internally, the Managing Server is composed of major pieces: The Xvfb (Virtual Frame Buffer) graphics package, DB2 UDB - or Oracle on Sun Solaris - as a relational data repository, WebSphere Application Server to run the WSAM GUI console application, an optional HTTP Web server (IBM Apache), and Cyanea overseer components which are a series of Java-based kernels and server routines.

The Cyanea overseer components are the controlling logic for the Managing Server itself. They are:

- The kernels control the Managing Server itself. There are always two copies of the kernels running on a WSAM Managing Server for redundancy and failover, registering components as they join the Managing Server, periodically renewing connections/registrations with components and data collectors, and collecting server and component availability information.
- The publishing servers receive application and system event data from the data collectors, gather and compute request-level information about performance metrics such as response times, and implement the trap monitoring and alerts features.

- The archive agents receive monitoring data from the publish servers, and stow the monitoring data in WSAM's repository.
- The global publishing server collects information from the publish servers, and correlates all parts and pieces of multi-server requests, like requests from J2EE servers to execute CICS programs.
- The message dispatcher is a conduit for messages from WSAM using EMAIL and SNMP facilities.
- The polling agents collect data from HTTP Web servers (Apache 2.0 and above servers only).
- The visualization engine is a Web-based GUI with access to graphics, WSAM performance reports, real-time views of different slices of monitoring data, and access to WSAM internal commands and event-driven functions.

1.3.2 The Data Collectors

The data collectors run inside the J2EE application servers and legacy servers. They use native system services, and they are tailored for the particular environments where they execute. The data collectors for z/OS systems are written to take advantage of services on z/OS, like MVS Cross-Memory Services and address space fencing, which are not available on distributed systems.

Data collectors have two agents: A *command agent* and an *event agent.*

The command agent fields requests from other components for information about EJB invocations, database connection pools, thread pools, stack traces, memory analyses, and heap dumps.

The event agent provides data to the publish servers according to polling frequencies. This data includes system initialization data, application request-level data, and application method-level data.

Collectively, these agents and other Data Collector routines unleash the probes, package the monitoring data into Java formats for the Managing Server, and deliver the data to the Managing Server.

The data collectors send the probes into JVMs and legacy servers to analyze their applications' performance. The probes collect monitoring data using standard system interfaces and APIs, and feed it to transport routines that in turn route the data to the Managing Server. The Managing Server processes that for display in the WSAM console and for storage in the WSAM repository. This removes as much of WSAM processing as possible from the JVMs and from legacy systems. The data collectors and probes are not designed to analyze or interpret data, but to collect it and route it as quickly as possible to the Managing Server where the analysis is then done there.

Data sources

The data sources employed by WSAM are:

- JVMTI GC data, method trace, stack trace, CPU time, and heap dump
- JMX system resources
- SMF system resources
- PMI system resources
- OS Services SCC, Platform CPU, and Environment

Once at the Managing Server, the monitoring data is prepared for real-time displays within the monitoring console and is inserted into the WSAM data repository. These are very resource-intensive operations; moving them to a standalone distributed server (or servers) isolates them from other enterprise activities, thus reducing WSAM's footprints in the monitored systems. This design also helps keep WSAM's processing overhead at levels low enough for 24x7 production system monitoring.

1.4 The three monitoring levels

WSAM fulfills multiple purposes and roles. It operates in testing and development systems to offer deep analyses of J2EE and legacy applications, tracking requests, nested requests, and application API calls to determine where bottlenecks exist in code. This kind of analysis, which can reach down to method, program, and API-level calls, requires a large footprint for the monitor itself, larger than can be sustained for extended monitoring in production systems.

This is no surprise. It is uniformly imperative for production systems that any monitoring tool has a very small footprint. If not, then the monitor's presence itself skews all the measurements and results gotten from it. WSAMs avoid this problem with variable footprints: There are production monitoring modes where the deep, intensive, method-level data capturing is bypassed. For these modes, monitoring is restricted to actions using the fewest resources themselves. Java classes by names or generic argument can be filtered from active monitoring too, further limiting the range of actions done by WSAM Data Collector probes in the production monitoring modes.

There are three monitoring levels in WSAM - L1, L2, and L3. Each successive level does more data capturing and so consumes more resources. L1 is the least intrusive level and captures information about user requests flowing through J2EE application servers, or transactions flowing through legacy systems like CICS and IMS. It is restricted to collecting request-level and transaction-level data only. L2 encompasses all of L1 plus collects information about nested requests, J2EE API or CICS/IMS API calls from applications for services delivered by the J2EE application or legacy system. An example of this is JDBC calls issued by applications to a relational database to extract, update, or store data. L3, the deepest level, includes all of L1 and L2 capabilities plus in-depth data gathering about method-level processing for J2EE applications and program-level processing for legacy systems. The CPU times and elapsed Internal times at entry to a method or program and at exit from a method or program are recorded. The Managing Server's routines then compute the times consumed by the method or program. Comparing these times for all the method or program invocations quickly identifies candidates for run-time improvements and code optimizations.

There is no instrumentation of application code by WSAM; data is collected at all three monitoring levels through JVM or legacy system features that support monitoring activities, like JVMTI for J2EE application servers and global user exit points for legacy systems. While WSAM's data collectors are optimized for the platforms on which they run, they do so only through standardized and published interfaces to operating system services on those platforms.

1.5 Monitoring methodologies

How and when WSAM is used depends very much on the environment in which it is installed and the particular problems at hand. For production systems, WSAM gauges the health of the server itself, its internal resources like CPU utilizations, JDBC connection pools, thread pools, and memory usage. In this production mode, WSAM can track requests as they flow through the server, offering up information about the number of requests, how long they take to complete, how many resources they consume, how many succeed or fail, and the in-flight status of active requests.

This last point is important: Computer operators are especially interested in the status of events executing in systems moment by moment, where hung or looping requests must be isolated, repaired, or removed from systems quickly. In its production modes, WSAM is particularly useful to operations, systems programming, and help desk staffs in identifying and resolving these kinds of real-time issues and problems.

L3 monitoring is useful in production systems too, where there is a need to analyze the performance of an application at method or program levels. L3 monitoring can be done in production systems, and there are times when it should be, but it should be used only sparingly and for very brief intervals or bursts. Once the data collection interval is over, WSAM should be reset to its typical production monitoring mode.

L3 monitoring is expected to be used more often in testing and development environments. There the tool is invaluable for applications' programming teams, offering in-depth analyses of J2EE and legacy applications that identify and isolate the Java methods and legacy programs that consume the most CPU times and elapsed internal times. Programmers can then bring other analytic tools into play to optimize the code running in these poorly performing routines.

1.5.1 In-flight request monitoring

In-flight request monitoring watches the real-time activities in a J2EE application server or a legacy system, tracking the status of requests as they execute. When requests appear to be unhealthy, perhaps hanging or looping out of control, they can be cancelled through direct operator intervention from WSAM's monitoring console.

1.5.2 Historical workload reporting

WSAM stows the monitoring data it collects in a relational database repository. The data stowed there can be archived and used for long-term comparisons and reporting. So, if a workload ran at certain levels and rates at one time, but seems to run differently now, the different sets of monitoring data collected for each session can be compared to determine exact differences and pinpoint likely causes for the changed behavior.

1.6 Request composite monitoring

Composite request monitoring offers up detailed traces of application events - reaching down into method-level or program-level analyses if necessary - connecting and correlating events that occur in one system with related events that occur in remote systems. These traces are thus "end-to-end" reports on a J2EE application's progress across hops to and from remote systems, regardless of how widely dispersed or distributed those systems might be.

In concrete terms, what this means is that the path of an application, analyzed as far down as the method-level or program-level, is reported from the time a user's request first arrives at the J2EE application server, then tracked across to the middleware transport layer, and tracked too within and across potentially multiple hops to back-end legacy systems, then back again to the originating or home J2EE application server through the middleware transport layer. All this activity is reported in the application traces as a single "unit-of-work." These traces bring an enterprise-wide, consolidated monitoring scope to distributed J2EE applications and legacy systems.

Composite request monitoring is based on application models in which requests are passed among programs running on the same or remote machines. Each request passes along a control block of information for the requested program to process. Responses from the called programs can be returned to the callers in the passed control block too. CICS technicians and architects will recognize this approach as being very similar to the External Call Interface (ECI) programming protocols and to IMS and WebSphere MQ messaging models.

When requests are processed in a J2EE application server that conforms to this model, and where either CICS Transaction Gateway, IMSConnect, or WebSphere MQ is used for data transport, then WSAM can correlate requests flowing between the J2EE application server and the legacy systems. WSAM can also track and correlate requests flowing between J2EE application servers (i.e., WebSphere-to-WebSphere) when the data transport between them is done by WebSphere MQ.

Composite request indicators appear in these four parts of the WSAM console:

- Server Activity displays of active requests/transactions on a server.
- In-Flight Request displays active requests/transactions for all servers, a group of servers, or specific servers.
- Performance Analysis and Reporting (PAR) detail reports are derived from Request/Transaction Analysis Trend reports. They offer views of the requests or transactions that appear on PAR Decomposition reports.
- Request Detail displays the details of requests or transactions, and provide controls for changing its status (if it is an active request/transaction).

See the *WSAM V3.1 User's Guide* for more information about these panels and reports.

1.6.1 Composite monitoring scope

To understand the scope of what WSAM monitors as composite requests, we introduce two terms: *managed space* and *composite request space.*

Managed space describes the entire scope of what WSAM can monitor. Since WSAM monitors HTTP Web servers, J2EE application servers, legacy systems, middleware transport tools, and J2EE applications and components like EJBs, the managed space can be quite complex.

Composite request space describes a subset of the managed space. Generally speaking, composite requests conform to an Enterprise Application Integration (EAI) architecture. They are requests to Web-enabled applications that flow through J2EE servers and legacy systems. The composite request space represents those parts of the WSAM managed space that participate in processing Web-enabled applications in J2EE servers and legacy systems.

A managed space is expected to have these resources:

- Servers : WSAM data collectors gather up platform-level data; any platform on which a Data Collector is installed is in the managed space. For z/OS systems, a server is considered to be equivalent to an LPAR.
- Application servers: WSAM data collectors obtain application server-level information. Any application server running in a JVM in which a Data Collector is installed is in the managed space. CICS and IMS systems are also considered to be application servers.
- Resources : WSAM monitors common resources that are available through the application server and J2EE APIs, such as EJB, JMS, JNDI, JDBC and JCA. If an application server is in the managed space, then the resources it provides and supports are also in the managed space.

- Applications: WSAM supports the monitoring of any application running in a J2EE application server or a legacy CICS or IMS system. If the application server or the legacy system is in the managed space, then the applications running in them are also in the managed space. Standalone applications which do not run in a J2EE application server or in a legacy CICS or IMS system are not in the managed space either.

1.6.2 Enterprise Application Integration

The fundamental notion of Enterprise Application Integration (EAI) is to make datastores and business processes in legacy systems accessible to Web-based networks and applications. From the J2EE perspective, this means that requests handled by J2EE application servers can invoke business processes or datastores in legacy systems through the J2EE Java Connection Architecture (JCA). WSAM also supports the IBM precursor to J2EE JCA, the Common Connection Framework (CCF). CCF is deprecated in favor of J2EE JCA, but it is still supported by WebSphere Application Server v5.1.

When describing correlations of EAI requests, the name home request is assigned to the initial J2EE request, and its application server is called the home server. A legacy transaction is a participating transaction, and its server is called a participating server. A J2EE application server that receives requests from home servers is also a participating server running participating requests. A home request may therefore have many related participating requests or transactions if the "unit-of-work" is parceled out to many servers.

A J2EE application server is in the managed space if a WSAM Data Collector is installed into it. If a legacy system is CICS, and a CSAM Data Collector is installed, then that system is within the managed space. Similarly, if the legacy system is IMS, and an ISAM Data Collector is installed, then that system is within the managed space.

Both the home request and participating requests always appear in WSAM's console. If the requirements for composite request monitoring are not met, then these requests appear independently of one another and there is no explicit indication that they are part of the same composite request or "unit-of-work".

1.6.3 CICS and IMS transactions in composite requests

Even though all transactions in CICS or IMS regions in the managed space appear in WSAM's console, they are not necessarily treated as parts of composite requests. A transaction in CICS or IMS can be correlated only if it meets these criteria:

- The legacy system is in the managed space.
- The home server is in the managed space.
- For CICS, the request on the home server must use External Call Interface (ECI) protocols through the CICS Transaction Gateway to execute CICS programs. This includes applications that use the IBM Common Connector Interfaces (CCI) as their JCA resource adapters, since CCI tools use ECI protocols.
- The ECI invocation is synchronous.
- The COMMAREA of the invoked CICS program must have at least 11 bytes of available room for the insertion of a token.
- For IMS: The application on the home server uses ICHJ to access IMSConnect.
- For CICS and IMS, the same rules apply for WebSphere MQ messages flowing between servers, except that the token is a logical one built up from data on WebSphere MQ message headers.

If any of these criteria are not met, then WSAM will not identify the request as a composite one. All information about the request as it flows through different servers in the managed space is recorded and reported, but none of the initial or subsequent related requests or transactions will be correlated with the initiating request.

For example, if a remote C++ application invokes a CICS program in the managed space through the CICS Transaction Gateway, the called CICS program appears in WSAM's console, but the remote C++ application and its call do not because WSAM does not monitor remote C++ applications. In this case, WSAM does not identify the called CICS program and its associated transaction as belonging to a composite request.

Likewise, if a Java application uses External Presentation Interface (EPI) protocols to execute CICS transactions, WSAM will not track the EAI request as a composite request, even if the application is in the managed space. In this case, the requests in the J2EE application server and the transactions in the CICS region both appear in WSAM's console, but they appear independently and are not identified as composite requests.

The stipulation about COMMAREAs is because of the method used by WSAM for tracking composite requests. WSAM places tiny tokens into COMMAREAs as they are passed from system to system. It is rare that programs use so much of COMMAREA storage that there is not enough room for WSAM's composite token. But, if and when these exceptional cases happen, WSAM does not identify the EAI request as a composite request, and the request's separate parts appear in WSAM's console only as independent, unrelated requests, or transactions running in their systems.

1.6.4 Multiple hops

Composite requests are not restricted to single-server transactions. In particular, composite requests include cases where CICS programs make Distributed Program Link (DPL) calls to other CICS regions. When such a call is made, the depth of the composite request increases. WSAM can track requests with no limit on the depth of these transaction "hops".

For IMS, any events with the same message tag from any IMS region in the IMS network appear as a single transaction. In addition, composite requests can include up to 100 participating requests made directly by each home or participating request. Although composite requests can include an unlimited depth of "hops", there is a limit on the number of trackable calls (spawned participating requests) made by any single request.

1.7 The install process in a nutshell

WSAM has a broad scope covering multiple platforms, diverse networks, relational databases, J2EE application servers, legacy transactional systems, and the operating systems on which they all run. This means that the installation and support of WSAM is usually a coordinated effort involving more than one software support team.

The next few paragraphs offer series of steps and waypoints for a typical WSAM installation. Follow these steps, or deviate from them only where site-level decisions demand it, and the installation will usually succeed without hands-on help from IBM WSAM support teams. These steps and waypoints are not meant to replace the detailed instructions in the following chapters or in the *WSAM Installation Guides*; they are high-level roadmaps through the install process itself.

So, do you want to install WSAM? Well, here is what you do:

1.7.1 Install and start the Managing Server

WSAM is a Managing Server (MS) and one or more data collectors (DCs). The Managing Server ought to be installed and fully operational before starting up any J2EE or legacy servers with a WSAM Data Collector. So the very first thing is to install the WSAM Managing Server. A Data Collector can be installed into a J2EE or legacy server before the MS is ready or in parallel, but then that server should not be started until after the WSAM MS is active.

The graphical installers require that the targeted MS host be enabled for Xwindows sessions and that a workstation have an Xwindows client like Hummingbird® Exceed or Cygwin. Otherwise, you must use a “silent” install or a manual install method.

Note: The WSAM MS can be installed across multiple boxes, putting different parts and pieces in remote places. This has the virtue of making the WSAM MS a genuinely scalable component, potentially supporting thousands of servers with WSAM data collectors. What we describe below is an installation of the MS on a single box. The WSAM V3.1 Install Guide has detailed instructions for constructing these environments.

The principal tasks on the MS host are:

- Get the distribution files and current maintenance for the WSAM MS major pieces: Xvfb (Virtual Frame Buffer), DB2 UDB, WebSphere Application Server, the IBM HTTP Web Server, and the Cyanea overseer Java components FTPed to the MS host.
- Define UNIX® userids and passwords for WSAM.
- Install the Xvfb package.
  - The JDK 1.4.x has a new property that eliminates the need for Xvfb to provide a graphical environment for WSAM's console.
- Install DB2 UDB v8.1 and Fix-pack 5 (graphical installer).
- Install WebSphere Application Server - Single Server Edition v5.1 (graphical installer).
- Install the IBM HTTP Web Server (optional, usually installed with WebSphere Application Server).
- Set permissions and database access privileges for the WSAM userids, “source” their profiles to activate the changes, and EXPORT some variables (WAS_HOME and JAVA_HOME, for example).
- Install the Cyanea overseer components (graphical installer). By default this process:
  - Builds the Octigate DB2 UDB database instance.
  - Builds the Cyanea WAS J2EE application server instance.
  - Builds the Cyanea overseer Java kernels and supporting server processes.
- Start the Managing Server by bringing up the major pieces sequentially.

Note: Remember that the sequence of starting up the WSAM MS major pieces makes a difference. Always start the pieces in this order: Xvfb, DB2 UDB, IBM HTTP Web Server (optional), WebSphere Application Server, and then the Cyanea overseer components. If possible, shut down a Managing Server by stopping the pieces in the reverse order. The MS post installation steps in the *WSAM V3.1 Install Guide* explain how to build a script for automating this startup sequence when the MS host is booted up.

- Sign on to the Managing Server's console from a Web browser.

If you can sign in to the WSAM Managing Server's console from your Web browser and navigate to the Configure Data Collectors panel, then you're ready to install and start your data collectors.

1.7.2 Install the Data Collectors

The data collectors go into J2EE application servers on distributed or z/OS systems, and into legacy CICS and IMS regions on z/OS systems.

If you are installing a distributed Data Collector, refer to Chapter 2 for pre-installation planning.

If you are installing a z/OS Data Collector, refer to Chapter 2 for pre-installation planning.

Installing the distributed Data Collectors

The distributed data collectors are installed through a graphical installer, so the process is pretty simple. The host for the J2EE application server to be monitored must be enabled for Xwindows sessions and your workstation must have an Xwindows client. Otherwise you must use a "silent" install method or a manual install method.

The installation steps are:

- Gather up the parameters and settings needed to run the graphical installer or the silent installer.
- Run the graphical installer or the silent installer.

Installing the z/OS Data Collectors

The very first thing to notice is that WebSphere Application Server v4 for z/OS is not supported by WSAM V3.1. You must be running WebSphere v5.0.2 or above on z/OS.

Many examples in this Redbook, and the examples to be found in the *WSAM V3.1 Install Manual*, usually refer to a temporary working directory for WSAM at /usr/lpp/tmp. You must ensure that both this working directory and the directory path where you will copy WSAM files for individual monitored servers (by default, /usr/lpp/cyanea) are acceptable as local names and as HFS mountpoint locations.

This bears repeating: The WSAM install process has three very important default directory paths. They are:

- /usr/lpp/tmp
- /usr/lpp/cyanea
- /opt/cyaneaone

The first is the temporary working directory where the WSAM MVS/USS-bound tar files are stored and untarred. The second is the location where configuration and environmental files for each monitored J2EE or legacy server are saved. Both these paths can be changed to suit local naming standards, but it's probably best if possible to use the default paths for the first z/OS Data Collector installation. The third path is the default installation path for the WSAM Managing Server. It too can be changed to suit local conventions and rules.

Note: You should consider the use of distinct mountpoints and separate HFSs to segregate WSAM files from all other files. At a minimum, we recommend that a separate HFS be created and mounted at the path /usr/lpp/cyanea. This will prevent MVS IPLs with new SYSRESs and new HFSs from causing any regression problems. The contents of the /usr/lpp/tmp subdirectories are to be copied to a permanent location (perhaps under /usr/lpp/cyanea/<wsam/cics/ims>/<wsam31/csam31/isam31>/), so there is no need for the temporary working directory after the first server installation is done.

Your next decisions are based on whether your WSAM V3.1 distribution is in an SMPe-installable format or in a non-SMPe format.

If you chose a non-SMPe distribution, then follow all the steps in the chapter for your Data Collector exactly, including the steps for FTPing the untarred contents of the *_DC_31_MVS.tar files to the host and reconstituting them as PDSs, and all the steps for FTPing the *_DC_31_USS.tar files to the host.

If you chose the SMPe-installable format, follow the steps of SMPe processing to populate the distribution and target datasets for WSAM V3.1. This process results in a set of MVS/PDS files and MVS/PDSe files on the mainframe host. You can skip any steps in your chapter about FTPing WSAM's non-SMPe-formatted distribution files to the MVS host. How many distribution datasets there are depends on the type of Data Collector being installed. Locate and confirm that you have all the PDS and PDSe files as described in the chapter for your Data Collector.

Install and start the CYN1 MVS subsystem

For any MVS LPAR on which a WSAM-monitored server is running, data is collected from WebSphere SM120 records and from the MVS Workload Manager (WLM) about performance goals if the CYN1 MVS subsystem is installed and running on that LPAR. The CYN1 subsystem is also used to allocate shared common storage needed for composite request monitoring.

Note: If you do not want to collect data from SMF120 records or WLM performance goals, or if you do not intend to activate composite request monitoring, then you can skip installing the CYN1 MVS subsystem.

CYN1 can be defined and activated either dynamically or statically. If the former, then an MVS IPL isn't needed to activate the changes to SYS1.PARMLIB members, for example. If the latter, then an IPL is needed. We recommend that CYN1 be installed both dynamically and statically, so that WSAM installers can proceed without needing an IPL and the changes are retained across subsequent IPLs.

The principal steps are:

- Get the distribution's MVS/PDS files from the untarred zWAS_DC_31_MVS.tar file FTPed to the mainframe host.
- Define the CYN1 MVS subsystem.
- Update the MVS security system.
- Update PROC00.
- APF-authorize SCYNAUTH and add to the MVS LNKLST.
- Define and install the IEFU83 SMF exit.
- Start the CYN1PROC.

z/OS steps

If you are installing a WSAM DC into a zWAS WebSphere J2EE server, then you should refer to *Installing WebSphere Studio Application Monitor V3.1*, SG24-6491.

If you are installing a CSAM or ISAM DC into a legacy system, then you must get the untarred contents of the CICS_DC_31_MVS.tar or the IMS_DC_31_MVS.tar files to the MVS host.

If you chose a non-SMPe-installable format, then follow all the steps in your chapter, including the steps for FTPing the untarred PDS files in *Installing WebSphere Studio Application Monitor V3.1*, SG24-6491.

If you chose an SMPe-installable format, then skip the steps in *Installing WebSphere Studio Application Monitor V3.1*, SG24-6491 about FTPing the distribution's MVS/PDS files to the MVS host. Locate the MVS/PDS files built from SMPe processing on your host and follow the remaining steps.

Note: The PDS library SCYNAUTH must be APF-authorized.

MVS/USS steps

If you chose a non-SMPe-installable format, then you must get the distribution's *_DC_31_USS.tar file FTPed to the MVS host. Follow the steps to FTP the PDSe files in your chapter exactly.

If you chose an SMPe-installable format, then skip the steps in your chapter about FTPing the distribution's *_DC_31_USS.tar file to the MVS host. Locate the *_DC_31_USS.tar file built from SMPe processing on the MVS host and follow the remaining steps.

- Un-tar the *_DC_31_USS.tar distribution file residing in /usr/lpp/tmp
  - This creates the subdirectories (depending on the type of server):
    - /cyanea/<wsam/cics/ims>/<cyanea_one/CICS1/IMS1>.
  - Subdirectories /lib, /etc, and /logs are built beneath /<cyanea_one/CICS1/IMS1> for all servers; a /bin directory is also built for the legacy data collectors.
- Build directories under /usr/lpp/cyanea:
  - /<wsam/cics/ims>/<server/APPLID/IMS ID> (with either the name of the J2EE server, the VTAM® APPLID of the CICS/TS region, or the name of the IMS system).
- Copy the files from the exploded temporary working directory:
  - cd to /usr/lpp/tmp/cyanea/<wsam/cics/ims>/<cyanea_one/CICS1/IMS1>
  - cp -R * /usr/lpp/cyanea/<wsam/csam/ims>/<server/APPLID/IMS ID>
- Change the directory and file permissions and ownerships as needed for your local security systems.
- Modify etc/datacollector.properties and etc/datacollector.env files.
  - Change the default MS IP addresses in datacollector.properties.
  - Change the default server name in the directory paths of datacollector.env.

Server steps

Server installation depends on the type of server.

- zWAS J2EE server
  - Update the zWebSphere PROCLIB statement in the server's startup JCL
  - Make configuration changes through the WAS admin console

- Required changes
- Optional changes

- CICS legacy server
  - Add WSAM PDSs to STEPLIB and DFHRPL
  - Add SIT table overrides
  - Update and reassemble the PLTPI table
  - Run DFHCSDUP to update the CICS CSD with CSAM's definitions in batch mode
- IMS legacy server
  - Add SCYNAUTH dataset to IMS control region's startup JCL before IMS RESLIB
  - APF-authorize /bin/imsprobe and /lib/libcyanea_imsvv_zos.so (vv is the IMS version number).
  - Add DDNAME CYNIMSIN and change the default directory path in the member if necessary.
  - Insert the ISAM IMS exit routines and concatenate with existing exit programs, if any.

1.7.3 Start the monitored servers

J2EE servers with WSAM and legacy systems with CSAM or ISAM start up without any changes to their operational procedures. Messages are displayed in the server's joblogs and in WSAM Data Collector logs about the success or failure of initializing the server and the Data Collector within it.

When a server is started with a Data Collector, two messages are displayed in the server's joblog:

- CYNK000I - PPEController...
- CYNK000I - PPEController...

The messages indicate that the collector successfully contacted the WSAM Managing Server and is ready to be configured for monitoring. There is one message for each kernel on the Managing Server.

If you do not see these messages in any JES2 joblogs, then something has gone wrong with initializing the Data Collector inside the server. Review the server's joblogs, the Data Collector logs, and if necessary, the Managing Server logs to diagnose and resolve the problem.

1.7.4 Configure the Data Collectors

Before a Data Collector can gather any data, it must be configured. This process is a manual one, requiring that an operator sign on to the WSAM Managing Server's console and configure the Data Collector the first time that a monitored server is started up with the Data Collector.

The steps are:

1. Sign on to the WSAM Managing Server console.
2. Click the Administration tab on the top navigation panel.
3. Select Server Management → Data Collector Configuration.
4. Choose the Unconfigured Data Collectors tab.
5. Apply a configuration setting to your Data Collector.

6. Return to the Data Collector Configuration panel and select the Configured Data Collectors tab.
7. The Data Collector should be present on the Configured Data Collectors panel.

If all goes well, you will see 2 messages in the server's JES2 joblogs, one for each of the Managing Server's kernels:

- CYNK0002I - PPEProbe...
- CYNK0002I - PPEProbe...

These messages indicate that the Data Collector is configured at the Managing Server and that the configuration information was transmitted successfully to the Data Collector.

Once the Data Collector is configured at the Managing Server console and these messages appear in the monitored server's joblogs, then monitoring data should start to appear in the WSAM console windows. Data collectors can be reconfigured at any time, but this manual process is not needed every time a server starts. Only the first time when the server starts with a WSAM DC installed, or possibly on the first startup after certain WSAM configuration files for the server are changed.

1.7.5 Verify the installation

To verify that the installation succeeded, it is generally sufficient to ensure that data collectors can register with the Managing Server and can be configured. If monitoring data appears in the WSAM console's windows, and PAR reports (historical performance reports) can be generated, then the installation is in pretty good shape.

1.7.6 Activate composite request monitoring

After WSAM is installed and the base features of the product are validated, then composite request monitoring can be activated too if desired.

First, ensure that the middleware transports are installed and operational, and that requests can flow through the home or originating servers, through the transports, and on into the targeted systems successfully. The transport middleware that can be used with WSAM composite monitoring is the IBM CICS Transaction Gateway, IBM IMSConnect, and IBM WebSphere MQ.

Once the transport middleware is engaged and the WSAM data collectors are installed and running in all home and participating servers, then the J2EE application servers can be updated to activate request composite monitoring.

Note: Once a CSAM or ISAM Data Collector is installed into a legacy CICS or IMS system, then no further steps must be taken to include traffic through that server in WSAM composite monitoring.

WAS-CTG-CICS monitoring

Follow these steps:

- In MVS/USS, update the .../etc/bcm.properties file for the home J2EE server to set ctg.enable=yes.
- Through the WAS admin console for the home J2EE server:
  - Ensure that the appserver.platform variables are set properly.

- Add the CICS Transaction Gateway's path to the directory /deployable (in which resides a cicseci.rar file) to the home server's LIBPATH.
- Update WSAM's custom probe service's CLASSPATH to include:
  - ${CONNECTOR_INSTALL_ROOT}/cicseci.rar:

- Configure and restart the Managing Server's publish servers and gps server, if necessary.
- Restart the J2EE application server.

WAS-MQ-CICS monitoring

Follow these steps:

- In MVS/USS, update the /etc/bcm.properties file for the home J2EE server to set mqi.enable=yes.
- Through the WAS admin console for the home J2EE server:
  - Ensure that the appserver.platform variables are set properly.
  - WebSphere MQ queue connection factories and queue destinations must be configured under the WebSphere MQ JMS Provider option.
  - Define a listener port for the MQI interface.
  - Update WSAM's custom probe service's CLASSPATH to include:
    - ${MQJMS_LIB_ROOT}/com.ibm.mq.jar:
- Configure and restart the Managing Server's publish servers and gps server, if necessary.
- Restart the J2EE application server.

Note: Additionally, when the J2EE server is configured with the WSAM Data Collector, you must indicate on the WSAM configuration panel that MQI traffic will flow through this server.

WAS-IMSConnect-IMS monitoring

Follow these steps:

- In MVS/USS, update the /etc/bcm.properties file for the home J2EE server to set imsconnect.enable=yes.
- Through the WAS admin console for the home J2EE server:
  - Ensure that appserver.platform variable is set properly.
  - Update WSAM's custom probe service's CLASSPATH to include:
    - ${CONNECTOR_INSTALL_ROOT}/imsico.rar/imseci.jar:
- Configure and restart the Managing Server's publish servers and gps server, if necessary.
- Restart the J2EE application server.

WAS-MQ-IMS monitoring

Follow these steps:

- In MVS/USS, update the /etc/bcm.properties file for the home J2EE server to set mqi.enable=yes.
- Through the WAS admin console for the targeted J2EE servers:
  - ensure that appserver.platform variable is set properly.

  - WebSphere MQ queue connections and queue destinations must be configured under the WebSphere MQ JMS Provider option.
  - Define a listener port for the MQI interface.
  - Update WSAM's custom probe service's CLASSPATH to include:
    - ${MQJMS_LIB_ROOT}/com.ibm.mq.jar:
- Configure and restart the Managing Server's publish servers and gps server, if necessary.
- Restart the J2EE application server.

> **Note:** Additionally, when the J2EE server is configured with the WSAM Data Collector, you must indicate on the WSAM configuration panel that MQI traffic will flow through this server.

J2EE-J2EE Monitoring

J2EE-J2EE monitoring occurs between two or more J2EE application servers. For each home and participating J2EE server, do the following:

- In MVS/USS, update the /etc/bcm.properties files for the J2EE servers to set mqi.enable=yes.
  - Ensure that appserver.platform variable is set properly.
- Through the WAS admin consoles for each J2EE server:
  - WebSphere MQ queue connections and queue destinations must be configured under the WebSphere MQ JMS Provider option.
  - Define a listener port for the MQI interface.
  - Update WSAM's custom probe service's CLASSPATH to include:
    - ${MQJMS_LIB_ROOT}/com.ibm.mq.jar:
- Configure and restart the Managing Server's publish servers and gps server, if necessary.
- Restart the J2EE application servers.

> **Note:** Additionally, when the J2EE servers are configured with the WSAM Data Collector you must indicate on the WSAM configuration panels that MQI traffic will flow through each server.

1.7.7 Post installation

So you're done and WSAM is working as it should. We recommend that you read Chapter 3, "Care and feeding of WSAM" on page 35 on the maintenance of WSAM. Building regular maintenance procedures for WSAM's monitoring repository and getting some familiarity with the Managing Server's operational commands are essential.

Chapter 5 has some guidelines on troubleshooting WSAM. Review them before contacting IBM personnel for assistance with problems that arise with installing or running WSAM.

2

Pre-installation planning

This chapter discusses planning items you need to consider before beginning the installation tasks for WebSphere Studio Application Monitor (WSAM).

© Copyright IBM Corp. 2005. All rights reserved.

2.1 Hardware and software prerequisites

Pre-installation planning is critical for a successful installation of WSAM.

Important: Please check the current product documentation for supported software release levels. It is very important to be sure you have the correct, supported release levels prior to starting your installation of WSAM. Unsupported release levels not only are high risk from a vendor product support point of view; they may not work at all, or some function may be missing. It is time well spent to be sure that all your prerequisite hardware and software is ready in advance.

2.1.1 Managing Server hardware

This section includes important considerations for managing your server hardware.

Sizing considerations

Sizing your Managing Server depends on a number of installation-specific variables, including the number of servers you wish to monitor, the transaction rates on those servers, the monitoring level (L1, L2, L3) of each, the request sampling rate you choose, and the amount of historical data reporting you do.

Ideally, you will work with IBM during production rollout planning to size the servers for your specific environment. There is an IBM-internal sizing tool which will give you an estimate of hardware requirements based upon your input. You may also choose to extrapolate from measurements in your test environment.

An informal internal test monitored an environment of 300,000 transactions per hour on a 2-processor pSeries® server. These were simple transactions, with predominantly L1 monitoring and very little other concurrent activity.

Keep in mind that functions such as L3 monitoring, high request sampling rates, and the historical Performance Analysis and Reporting are the most resource intensive. The more of these you do concurrently, the larger the configuration you will need. In particular, the depth of the methods executed by your applications contributes significantly to the overhead and to the amount of DB2 space needed to store them (L3). Also keep in mind other requirements, such as redundancy for high availability environments.

Preliminary requirements

The following guidelines, as shown in Table 2.1, provide a suggested starting point for a pre-production environment. The Managing Server may be installed on various hardware platforms. Choosing which platform is right for you mostly involves selecting a system which is familiar to your systems programming support teams. The sizing of the Managing Server should be done initially with an IBM IT Architect or IT Specialist familiar with WSAM. They will gather up specific information about your environment to be monitored and then they will provide you with guidance on how many system resources (CPUs, memory, and disk) are needed to match your planned usage of WSAM.

Table 2-1 Preliminary Managing Server hardware configuration

	CPU	DISK	MEMORY
AIX® 5L™	4 way	3 x 36 GB	4 GB

	CPU	DISK	MEMORY
Intel/Linux®: RHEL 2.1AS	4 way	3 x 36 GB	4 GB
Solaris 8	4 way	3 x 36 GB	4 GB

2.1.2 Managing Server software

The Managing Server is a standalone server or a collection of servers. That is, you can choose to install the following components on separate, dedicated servers for scalability or availability reasons. However, for most customers, the best practice is to run the Managing Server on one dedicated box, with no other applications on it.

It consists of the following elements:

- Database – to store performance data and configuration information.
- J2EE Application Server – to run the monitoring console.
- Java Components – The Managing Server consists of several components, each of which runs as a Java process, including the following: Kernel, Publish Server, Archive Agent, Message Dispatcher, Polling Agent, Global Publish Server, and the Port Consolidator.

You must have a supported combination of operating system platform, database, and application server in order to use the Managing Server. Table 2-2 describes the supported combinations.

Table 2-2 Supported environments for the WSAM Managing Server

Operating System	Database	Application Server	JDK
AIX 5.1	DB2 UDB v8.1 Fixpack 5	WebSphere 5.1.1	Supplied by Application Server
AIX 5.2	DB2 UDB v8.1 Fixpack 5	WebSphere 5.1.1	Supplied by Application Server
Intel/Linux: RHEL 2.1AS	DB2 UDB v8.1 Fixpack 5	WebSphere 5.1.1	Supplied by Application Server
Solaris 8	DB2 UDB v8.1 Fixpack 5	WebSphere 5.1.1	Supplied by Application Server
Solaris 8	Oracle 8.1.7	WebSphere 5.1.1 or WebLogic 8.1 sp3	Supplied by Application Server
Solaris 9	Oracle v10g	WebSphere 5.1.1	Supplied by Application Server
Linux for zSeries: SuSe Linux 8.1	DB2 UDB v8.1 Fixpack 5	WebSphere 5.1.1	Supplied by Application Server

HTTP server

If you want to have the WSAM Web console run on port 80, you need to install and configure an HTTP server to serve those requests. You can find the instructions in Appendix E of the *WSAM Installation Guide*.

Virtual frame buffer

The Managing Server requires a graphical environment to support many of the pages your users want to view in WSAM. In the past, this required Virtual Frame Buffer software to be installed and running on your Managing Server.

With the implementation of JDK 1.4.x, there is a new property that removes the need for starting a new Xserver with Virtual Frame Buffer to provide the graphical environment we need. The variable is:

java.awt.headless=true

In the WebSphere Administrative Console, go to:

Application Servers →Cyanea →Process Definition →Java Virtual Machine

Also, create/update this property with the value of "`true`". Then recycle the server.

If necessary, you can also install the following package as appropriate for your operating system.

For Red Hat Linux: Install the XFree86-Xvfb package. You can find this on your Red Hat Linux CD or at:

`http://www.redhat.com`

For AIX: Install the Virtual Frame Buffer (xvfb). This package can be found on the AIX installation CD X11.vfb package ("Virtual Frame Buffer Software for AIX Windows®") from the AIX CD.

For Solaris: Install from the x11 distribution.

For Linux for zSeries: Install from the x11 distribution.

2.1.3 Data Collector hardware

The WSAM Data Collector runs on your existing WebSphere Application Server systems. No additional hardware is required, but you may want to increase the heap size by 64 MB above the current configuration in UNIX and Windows environments, especially if your heap is already constrained.

2.1.4 Data Collector software

Next is described Data Collector software requirements. This set of defined environments were the environments used for initial certification of the current release of the WSAM product. Subsequent to GA ongoing testing has continued and additional environments are supported. Please check with your IBM representative for the most current supported environments.

Distributed environments (UNIX and Windows)

The following, as shown in Table 2-3, are the software requirements for the Data Collector on distributed platforms.

Table 2-3 Supported environments for the WSAM Data Collector

Platform	Application server	Additional requirements
AIX 5.1	WebSphere 5.0.2.6, 5.1.1 WebSphere Portal 5.0.2	Check that the following packages are installed. (The numbers may be these or later file set numbers.) ► bos.perf.diag_tool 5.1.0.25 Performance Diagnostic Tool ► bos.perf.libperfstat 5.1.0.35 Performance Statistics Library ► bos.perf.perfstat 5.1.0.36 Performance Statistics Interface ► bos.perf.tools 5.1.0.35 Base Performance Tools
AIX 5.2	WebSphere 5.0.2.6, 5.1.1	Check that the following packages are installed. (The numbers may be these or later file set numbers.) ► bos.perf.diag_tool 5.2.012 Performance Diagnostic Tool ► bos.perf.libperfstat 5.2.0.10 Performance Statistics Library ► bos.perf.perfstat 5.2.0.14 Performance Statistics Interface ► bos.perf.tools 5.2.0.17 Base Performance Tools
Solaris 8	WebSphere 5.0.2.6, 5.1.1	
Solaris 9	WebSphere 5.0.2.6, 5.1.1	
HP-UX 11.iv1	WebSphere 5.0.2.6, 5.1.1	In order to generate a Java heap dump, you must rebuild the kernel. See “Rebuild the HP-UX Kernel” on page 103 of the Installation Guide.
Windows 2000 sp4	WebSphere 5.0.2.6, 5.1.1	
Windows 2003	WebSphere 5.0.2.6, 5.1.1	
RHEL 2.1 (Intel®)	WebSphere 5.0.2.6, 5.1.1	
Linux for zSeries SuSe 8.1	WebSphere 5.0.2.6, 5.1.1	

z/OS

The following, as shown in Table 2-4, are the software requirements for the Data Collector on z/OS WebSphere (note: Linux for zSeries is in the prior chart).

Table 2-4 Supported environments for the z/OS Data Collector

Operating System	Application Server	JDK	Optional Software
z/OS 1.2 - 1.6	WebSphere 5.0.2.012, 5.1.0.003	JDK 1.3 (cm131s-20040117) for WebSphere 5.0.2 JDK 1.4 (cm1411sr2a-20040515) for WebSphere 5.1	MQ5.3.1, DB2 7.1 (0311), DB2 7.0 Universal Driver

CICS

You can install and configure CSAM V3.1 data collectors on systems with the following specifications:

- z/OS v1.2, v1.3, or v1.4
- CICS Transaction Server for z/OS v1.3, v2.2, or v2.3
- One or more LPARs (CICS v2.3 does not work on less than z/OS v1.4.)

In addition, in order to use the composite request features of WSAM and CSAM, you must configure one or more data collectors that monitor J2EE requests, from among the following application server/platform combinations:

- WebSphere 5.1 on z/OS 1.2 (and above), AIX 5L or Solaris 8

There are some additional restrictions. Please see 2.8 for more details.

IMS

You can install and configure IMS Data Collectors on systems with the following specifications:

- z/OS 1.2, 1.3, or 1.4
- IMS for z/OS version 7.1 with a minimum put level 0401, 8.1, or 9.1
- One or more LPARs

In addition, in order to use the composite request features of WSAM and ISAM, you must configure one or more data collectors that monitor J2EE requests, from among the following application server/platform combinations:

- • WebSphere 5.1 on z/OS 1.2 (and above), AIX 5L or Solaris 8

There are some additional restrictions. Please see 2.8 for more details.

2.2 Managing Server configuration options

Some decisions must be made about the WSAM Managing Server. How many, and how do you want to configure them?

2.2.1 How many?

The term WSAM managed space introduced in Chapter 1 can be understood to refer to all J2EE servers and legacy systems whose data collectors are controlled by the same WSAM Managing Server. There is a one-to-many relationship between managing servers and data collectors, and there is a many-to-one relationship between data collectors and managing servers. A Data Collector can register with only one Managing Server at a time.

It is easy to build multiple, completely independent managed spaces, the most obvious example of this is a separation of production servers from test/development servers. There are several reasons why having a production managed space and a test/development managed space are a good idea:

- Each Managing Server and therefore each managed space has its own monitoring repository. Decisions about how, when, and whether that data is archived or deleted might be different for production-derived data than for test/development data. Using two repositories means that the procedures about persisting the data can be tailored for each database.
- Monitoring demands for production systems are different from those for test/development systems. Each successive level of WSAM monitoring raises the quantity of data stored in the WSAM repository. For production systems, the amount of data to be transported ought to be minimized; for test/development systems this shouldn't be an issue. Two managing servers and two repositories mean that the production repository need not be filled with quantities of data from testing environments, and the testing repository need not be hampered by unwanted limitations for speedy performance.
- Operational procedures and practices are different for production resources than they are for test/development resources. Two repositories fit into this structure better than one.

If your infrastructure has and wants clear, sharp boundaries between production systems and test/development systems, then you are likely to be better served by segregating the servers into different managed spaces.

2.2.2 Managing Server topologies

The WSAM Managing Server is designed with loosely coupled components and processes. All the parts and pieces can reside on one box, or they can be split out among many boxes. For example:

- The WebSphere Application Server and DB2 UDB could be on one box and the overseer components on another.
- The WebSphere Application Server could be on one box, DB2 UDB on another, and the overseer components on a third box.
- The overseer components generally communicate with one another using TCP sockets, so the components themselves can be spread out among many boxes.
- The number of components can be increased too. So, if more than two publish servers are needed to handle data transport between data collectors and a Managing Server, more publish servers can be started.

Figure 2-1 is an illustration of a multi-box Managing Server installation. This scenario has WebSphere Application Server and the Cyanea overseer components clustered horizontally over two nodes with a remote database and a load balancer in front:

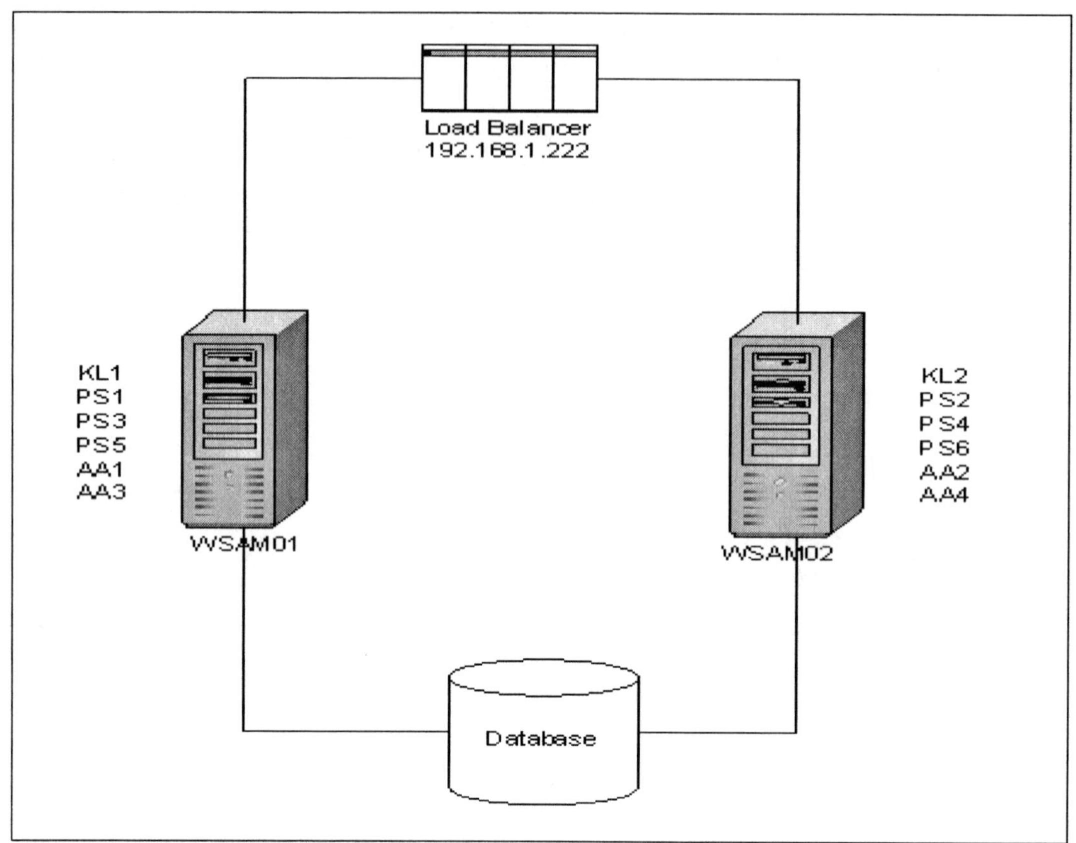

Figure 2-1 Multi-Box Managing Server

All these possibilities make for many and varied WSAM managed space configurations, with many ways to scale WSAM into virtually any environment and workload, large or small.

2.3 Data Collector considerations

z/OS HFS

As files initially are generated to the /<installation directory>/wsam/<server>/etc directory and ongoing to the /<installation directory>/wsam/<server>/logs directory, these directories must be READ-WRITE. This may be accomplished by mounting a unique HFS file over the /<installation directory>/wsam/<server>/ directory or by creating a symbolic link that will redirect access from the /<installation directory>/wsam/<server>/logs and /<installation directory>/wsam/<server>/etc directories to another set of directories that are READ-WRITE.

If you have a shared HFS environment, keep in mind that files will be written to your WSAM /etc and /log subdirectories for each server you are monitoring. Your WSAM /bin directory will contain the executables, which you may want to share among a set of servers, with different levels as you roll new releases of WSAM through your environment.

We used the following naming conventions for our z/OS WebSphere Data Collector files:

- /usr/lpp/cyanea/wsam/jdsr04a/etc
- /usr/lpp/cyanea/wsam/jdsr04a/lib
- /usr/lpp/cyanea/wsam/jdsr04a/logs

Here, jdsr04a is one of our server names (see section on plan your hfs WSAM naming convention).

Place your /etc and /logs directories with an eye to write performance if you are sharing your hfs. Use symbolic links to direct to an hfs on the LPAR where your Data Collector resides so you don't have the performance penalty of routing each write to the owning system in a shared hfs. The following URL has several good Parallel Sysplex® Test Report documents which discuss hfs and zFS setup:

```
http://www-1.ibm.com/servers/eserver/zseries/zos/integtst/library.html
```

2.4 Network and protocol considerations

The servers on which the Managing Server is installed must have a real hostname and IP address (rather than just using localhost or 127.0.0.1.).

For a z/OS WebSphere Data Collector, if your LPAR has more than one IP address, make sure your system and/or network (DNS) are configured such that the primary IP is used for all connections between the Data Collector and Managing Server. You can use the netstat-command to check the IPs used. Or, you may specify the IP to be used by Application Monitor in the WebSphere configuration via the java.rmi.server.hostname parameter in JVM Servant properties in z/OS WebSphere version 5.

2.5 Firewalls

If a firewall sits between your Managing Server and your Data Collectors, you must configure your firewall to allow these connections.

Data Collectors use eight ports to communicate with the Managing Server: Six ports for TCP/IP sockets, and two ports for RMI. In addition, two unique ports are needed for each Data Collector, in order for the Managing Server to contact the Data Collectors via RMI.

Follow the instructions below to configure the firewall between the Managing Server and the Data Collector (if you do not have a firewall between your Managing Server and your Data Collector, please ignore these instructions).

To configure your firewall:

1. Open the following ports on the firewall from both directions: 9103-9104 9111 9118-9123 9126 9129 9130 8300-83xx 8200-82xx. (Assuming you used the default settings.)
2. Update the datacollector.properties file (on the machine running the Data Collector). This is typically located at /opt/cyaneaone/etc (the installation directory):

   probe.rmi.port=8300

   probe.controller.rmi.port=8200
3. If there is more than one Data Collector installed on a node, you must open a port for each Data Collector in both ranges starting from 8200 and 8300. Then assign unique values for each in the respective datacollector.properties files.

Note: You can use the optional component, Port Consolidator, to minimize the number of ports required. See the *Operator's Guide, Appendix C. Port Consolidator.*

2.6 Repository database sizing

The WSAM database repository is DB2 UDB or Oracle on Sun Solaris. Both use the same relational data model. Sizing the database is an exercise in estimating an average workload's requirements per day and then multiplying that number by the number of days the data is to be retained in the database.

As part of the pre-installation process, WSAM Services and Support will ask you to provide these estimates to them:

- What is the number of users/sessions (users) per day (farm wide)?
- What is the number of requests per session?
- What sampling rates to be are used?
- How many servers are to be run at L3 monitoring?
- How often do garbage collections occur per minute?
- What polling interval will you use for monitoring (the default is 60 seconds)?
- How many days of history are to be retained before archiving or deleting the data?

These estimates are then used to calculate the optimum database size for your site.

2.7 DB2 drivers

WSAM supports both of the following drivers:

- DB2 for z/OS Local JDBC Provider (RRS on z/OS)
- DB2 Universal JDBC Driver Provider

2.8 Legacy systems for composite request monitoring

WSAM, CSAM and ISAM merge together requests that flow between servers, correlating the requests' activities in one server with their activities in others. This includes the requests' activities in the legacy transaction servers CICS/TS and IMS.

2.8.1 CICS

CICS v1.3, v2.2, and v2.3 can participate in composite monitoring when the middleware transport vehicle is the CICS Transaction Gateway.

CICS v2.2. and v2.3 can participate in composite monitoring when the transport vehicle is WebSphere MQ.

2.8.2 IMS

IMS v7.1, v8.1 and v9.1 on z/OS can participate in composite monitoring when the middleware transport vehicle is either IMSConnect or WebSphere MQ.

2.9 Middleware for composite request monitoring

WSAM's composite request monitoring works with the CICS Transaction Gateway, IMSConnect, or WebSphere MQ. All three products are used as transport mechanisms between servers. For CICS/TS systems, requests conforming to External Call Interface (ECI) programming protocols are tracked as they traverse servers and systems.

For IMS and WebSphere MQ, message-driven models lie at their center and WSAM correlates the message traffic across servers and systems.

Note that you need to run the CYN1 proc to enable composite request monitoring, since it allocates required working storage. See chapter 6 for more information on installing and running CYN1.

2.9.1 CICS Transaction Gateway

The CICS Transaction Gateway is a separately orderable software package. It enables remote Java applications to call certain kinds of programs running in CICS/TS systems. The called programs must conform to the CICS Distributed Program Link (DPL) model. In this application model, requests are passed between servers with a "commarea" of data transferred back and forth too. The commarea is the data that the called program is to process and - if desired - return results to the caller.

When traffic flows between a WSAM-monitored J2EE server to the CICS Transaction Gateway and then on to a CSAM-monitored CICS/TS system using ECI protocols, WSAM and CSAM can correlate the activities in the servers together, marking out the entire path of the request.

The CICS Transaction Gateway v5.0, v5.0.1, or .v5.1 is required.

2.9.2 IMSConnect

IMSConnect is handled by WSAM and ISAM in precisely the same way that the CICS Transaction Gateway is handled by WSAM and CSAM. IMSConnect and the CICS Transaction Gateway are both transport vehicles.

Since IMS employs a message-driven processing model, IMSConnect follows in that path and the traffic routed by IMSConnect is composed of messages sent between servers. WSAM and ISAM operate in this environment by correlating messages as they flow through different servers. So, a message generated by a servlet perhaps in a J2EE server and destined for an IMS system, if it is transported there by IMSConnect, can be tracked by WSAM and ISAM as each server processes its part of the message and passes it on.

IMSConnect v2.1 or v2.2 is required.

2.9.3 WebSphere MQ

WebSphere MQ also employs a message-driven processing model. In this respect, WSAM monitoring, where WebSphere MQ is involved as the transport vehicle, is again at the message level. There is no inherent transactional context to the data being transported between servers.

WebSphere MQ v5.3.1 is required.

Customization

Given the prerequisite software levels as listed in this chapter, there is no customization required in MQ to do composite monitoring of transactions using MQ as the transport mechanism. You do need to perform the customization steps for Adding MQI Capturing Support for WebSphere and edit the bcm.properties file (see later sections of this book for your appropriate Data Collector).

However, you do have to install Data Collectors in each subsystem your transactions access, such as WebSphere, CICS, or IMS. Keep in mind that correlation is only meaningful between two (or more) execution environments, such as WebSphere-to-CICS via MQ, WebSphere-to-IMS via MQ, or WebSphere-to-WebSphere via MQ.

With Data Collectors in each subsystem, WSAM will be able to report on the entire flow of the transaction within each subsystem and across MQ.

2.10 Composite request monitoring requirements tables

Tables 2-5 through 2-11 summarize the supported environments for composite request monitoring. In general, you need:

- CICS 1.3, 2.2, or 2.3
- CTG 5.0, 5.0.1, or 5.1
- IMS 7.1, 8.1, or 9.1
- IMS Connect 2.1 or 2.2
- MQ 5.3.1
- WebSphere 5.0.2 or 5.1

Check the tables from Table 2-5 through Table 2-11 on page 33 for your operating environment in order to determine the specific combination of supported software.

Table 2-5 Composite request requirements for CICS Data Collector using CTG

Operating System	Application Server	CTG Version
z/OS 1.3 - 1.4	CICS 1.3 or 2.2	5.0 or 5.0.1
z/OS 1.4	CICS 2.3	5.0.1 or 5.1

Table 2-6 Composite request requirements for CICS Data Collector using MQ

Operating System	Application Server	MQ Version
z/OS 1.3 - 1.4	CICS 2.2	5.3.1
z/OS 1.4	CICS 2.3	5.3.1

Table 2-7 Composite request requirements for J2EE Data Collector using CTG

Operating System	Application Server	CTG Version
z/OS 1.2 - 1.4	WebSphere 5.0.2 and 5.1	5.0.1 or 5.1
AIX	WebSphere 5.0.2 and 5.1	5.0.1 or 5.1
Solaris	WebSphere 5.0.2 and 5.1	5.0.1 or 5.1

Table 2-8 Composite request requirements for J2EE Data Collector using MQ

Operating System	Application Server	MQ Version
z/OS 1.3 - 1.4	WebSphere 5.0.2 and 5.1	5.3.1
AIX	WebSphere 5.1	5.3.1
Solaris	WebSphere 5.1	5.3.1

Table 2-9 Composite request requirements for IMS Data Collector using IMS Connect

Operating System	Application Server	IMS Connect Version
z/OS 1.2 - 1.4	IMS 7.1, 8.1, or 9.1	2.1 or 2.2

Table 2-10 Composite request requirements for IMS Data Collector using MQ

Operating System	Application Server	MQ Version
z/OS 1.2 - 1.4	IMS 7.1, 8.1, or 9.1	5.3.1

Table 2-11 Composite request requirements for J2EE Data Collector using IMS Connect

Operating System	Application Server	IMS Connect Version
z/OS 1.2 - 1.4	WebSphere 5.0.2 and 5.1	2.1 or 2.2

Care and feeding of WSAM

WSAM runs on multiple platforms in networked environments and employs a relational database to store monitoring data. All these features require that you handle WSAM with clearly defined, ongoing maintenance and support procedures. Neglect the topics in this chapter, and WSAM will almost certainly develop problems. Follow the guidelines outlined here, and WSAM will perform its monitoring functions with minimal intrusions on workload processing.

In particular, you must manage the relational database like any relational database, with periodic observation and tuning by operations and systems personnel. This role is familiar to mainframe DB2 administrative and systems personnel. You should copy or modify the procedures you employ for databases on mainframe systems for applicability to the WSAM Managing Server.

You can run WSAM in high-volume workload environments where potentially thousands or hundreds of thousands of methods are invoked by single requests. This kind of processing places special demands on WSAM and its resources. We offer explanations about those tuning parameters that ought to be engaged to handle these situations.

And last, WSAM, especially its Managing Server, is a complex apparatus and how it is managed day-to-day is critical to the success of WSAM in an enterprise. We describe typical operational duties and the console commands that engage them.

© Copyright IBM Corp. 2005. All rights reserved.

3.1 Repository maintenance

The WSAM repository is typically a DB2 UDB system. WSAM's repository needs all the care and attention that any repository of enterprise-valuable data would demand. The monitoring data collected by WSAM is stored in this repository. How valuable that data is and how long it must persist are decisions for each customer. If the data is judged to be non-persistent, so that there is no need to archive any data, then cleaning the database tables periodically will suffice.

On the other hand, if you need to retain the monitoring data for historical analyses, then archival and backup procedures are needed to ensure that the data persists as expected. These routines and procedures are familiar to all mainframe DB2 personnel. They should be placed into the WSAM Managing Server environment, too.

The script run-stat-cmds.sh is provided as a command line utility so that users can schedule CRON jobs to periodically maintain the database. Execute run-statcmds.sh daily. If there is still a performance problem in the Performance Analysis and Reporting, then perform the following procedures:

The data maintenance utilities are as follows:

- REORGCHK
- REORG
- RUNSTAT

To perform data maintenance on the database:

1. Login to WSAM db2 server.
2. DB2 connect to octigate user db2inst1.
3. DB2 reorgchk update statistics on table <cyanea.tablename>. (Go to step 4 and 5 or table reorganization if an asterisk is shown in the REORG column of the output. Otherwise, skip the steps.)
4. DB2 reorg table <cyanea.tablename> index <cyanea.indexname>.
5. DB2 RUNSTAT on table <cyanea.tablename>.

While the database tables are being reorganized, the WSAM archive agent component cannot insert any monitoring data into the database tables. Therefore, reorganization and data trimming activities should always be done when there are minimal needs for the monitoring of systems and servers.

The Data Trimmer

Use the Data Trimmer to trim old data that does not need to be maintained in the database any longer. It is provided as a command line utility so that users can schedule CRON jobs to trim data periodically.

Note: Be aware that running this command could take a very long time depending on the amount of data being trimmed.

The syntax is:

```
/opt/cyaneaone/bin/dataTrimmer.sh dbuser dbpassword startdate starttime enddate endtime
[maxrow]
```

starttime and endtime must be specified using military (24-hour) notation. The optional parameter maxRow is the number of rows committed to the database in a transaction. The default for maxRow is 1000.

For example, to delete data collected from January 1 2003 to March 31 2003, use the following invocation:

```
/opt/cyaneaone/bin/dataTrimmer.sh dbuser dbpassword 01/01/03 00:00:00 03/31/03 11:59:59
```

The Data Trimmer is used to trim old, unnecessary data from the WSAM repository. For REQUEST and METHOD tables, this process has two parts: marking records to be deleted and deleting marked records.

This release of the Data Trimmer does not support more than one instance of the trimmer running concurrently. To support more that one instance of the trimmer running concurrently, you need to use the cyanea user account, and you should make the properties file accessible to the cyanea user. You need the following files to use the Data Trimmer:

- $CYANEA_HOME/lib/datatrim.jar
- $CYANEA_HOME/etc/datatrim.xml
- $CYANEA_HOME/etc/markdatadeleting.xml
- $CYANEA_HOME/bin/datatrim.sh

The Data Trimmer will produce the following file after it runs:

- $CYANEA_HOME/logs/datatrim.log

To execute the Data Trimmer:

1. Start the Data Trimmer process on the Managing Server (If you have your Managing Server and Database Server on two different machines, start the Data Trimmer on the Managing Server machine.). The syntax is:

   ```
   $CYANEA_HOME/bin/datatrim.sh <dbname> <dbuser> <dbpassword>
   ```

   Where the dbname is the WSAM database name, dbuser and dbpassword combination will allow the Data Trimmer to access the WSAM database.

2. The process log file is located under:

   ```
   $CYANEA_HOME/logs/datatrim.log
   ```

3. The default JVM minimum heap size is 128 and the maximum is 256. You can increase the JVM heap size in datatrim.sh for optimum performance.
4. See the property files (markdatadeleting.xml and datatrim.xml) to setup the parameters.
5. In case of failure, rerun the datatrim.sh script.

Data Trimmer properties files

The markdatadeleting.xml file is found in the <CYANEA_HOME>/etc directory. To schedule deleting records in the REQUEST and METHOD tables, set the following properties:

- commitcount
  - Number of records to be committed to database in a transaction (commitcount). The default for commitcount is 500. This number should be set to a number lower than the maximum number of locks allowed to be held per transaction.
- useoracle
  - Indicator of database type (useoracle). The default for useoracle is false. If an Oracle database is used, then the value should be true.

- daystokeep
  - Number of days to keep the data (daystokeep). If you want to trim all data up to 7 days ago, then daystokeep=7. For example, if today is July 8, 2004, and you specify daystokeep=7, the Data Trimmer will do the following:
    - Find out what the current date is (July 8, 2004).
    - Keep today's data.
    - Start counting 7 days back from 24 hours ago yesterday (July 7, 2004) – July 1st, 2004.
    - Delete all data up to June 30th, 2004, inclusive.
    - Data from July 1st onwards is kept.
- startdate
  - Start date for deleting data (startdate). Use this to specify a time period for deleting data. To delete from and not include January 1 2003, enter startDate= 01/01/03 00:00:00. If "daystokeep" property is specified, then this property will not be used.
- enddate
  - End date for deleting data (enddate). Use this to specify a time period for deleting data. To delete up to and not including March 31, 2003, enter endDate=03/31/03 00:00:00. If "daystokeep" property is specified, then this property will not be used.

The datatrim.xml file is found in the <CYANEA_HOME>/etc directory. To schedule deleting records in the database, set the following properties:

Properties that apply to all tables:

- commitcount
  - Number of records to commit to database in a transaction (commitcount). The default for commitcount is 500. This number should be set to a number lower than the maximum number of locks allowed to be held per transaction.
- useoracle
  - Indicator of a database type (useoracle). The default for useoracle is false. If an Oracle database is used, then the value is true.

Properties that apply to each individual table, such as PMISTATS, SERVERSTATS, and VOLUMESTAT:

- daystokeep
  - Number of days to keep the data (daystokeep). If you want to trim all data up to 7 days ago, then daystokeep=7. For example, if today is July 8, 2004, and you specify daystokeep=7, the Data Trimmer will do the following:
    - Find out what the current date is (July 8, 2004)
    - Keep today's data
    - Start counting 7 days back from 24 hours ago yesterday (July 7, 2004) – July 1st, 2004
    - • Delete all data up to June 30th, 2004, inclusive
    - • Data from July 1st onwards is kept

- startdate
  - Start date for deleting data (startdate). Use this to specify a time period for deleting data. To delete from and not include January 1 2003, enter startDate= 01/01/03 00:00:00. If "daystokeep" property is specified, then this property will not be used.
- enddate
  - End date for deleting data (enddate). Use this to specify a time period for deleting data. To delete up to and not including March 31, 2003, enter endDate=03/31/03 00:00:00. If "daystokeep" property is specified, then this property will not be used.

3.2 High-volume tuning

WSAM is designed for high-volume workloads. This can mean either running in environments with large volumes of J2EE requests or environments with individual J2EE requests that call many thousands or hundreds of thousands of methods to do their work.

Workloads with large request volumes

For z/OS environments that run workloads with large request volumes, the WSAM WebSphere Data Collector for z/OS is tailored to the z/OS environment itself. The Data Collector's probes run as a custom service to WebSphere Application Server, gathering the PMI data produced by WebSphere, and invoking JVMTI function primitives to obtain other information about processes and requests running in the J2EE server's JVM. There is no instrumentation of application code by WSAM: All monitoring data is captured using established, standard monitoring APIs and services.

SMF 120 record data and MVS Workload Manager (WLM) performance data are captured too. This is done by an MVS subsystem running in parallel with the WSAM-monitored servers. The MVS subsystem watches the MVS IEFU83 exit point and intercepts traffic from there to obtain SMF 120 records. WLM performance data is obtained from functions running inside the MVS subsystem itself. The monitoring data is sent via MVS Cross-Memory Services to WSAM native routines running on behalf of the WSAM-monitored J2EE server. The routines then ship the data across RMI/IIOP connections to the WSAM Managing Server and into the monitoring repository.

The data collectors and their probes are designed to run with minimal impact to the host. The collectors ship data to the Managing Server in a continuous stream. It is on the Managing Server that the data is processed: It is prepared for insertion into the monitoring repository and it is prepared for real-time display in the WSSAM console. Moving those functions to the distributed Managing Server removes them from the systems with data collectors installed. This significantly reduces resource demands by WSAM data collectors.

Provided the WSAM monitoring levels are used judiciously, and class-level filters are employed where appropriate, it is unlikely that WSAM will require special treatment for these environments. Usual tuning practices for software on z/OS platforms should be followed, of course.

The WSAM monitoring levels and filters act as brakes on the use of the probes to collect data, thus reducing the CPU utilization levels they incur. The sampling rates for data collectors act as brakes on the amount of data stowed in the repository, thus reducing demands on that resource. Memory allocations on all systems should be checked occasionally to ensure that paging rates are acceptable when running WSAM-monitored J2EE workloads at peak capacities.

Requests with large method volumes

A single J2EE request can call thousands or hundreds of thousands of methods. At the L3 monitoring level, WSAM records the entry and exit to each method along with the CPU times and elapsed internal times for the currently executing thread at those points. From these events, request traces are built, identifying the progress of an application through its methods as they are invoked and exited. When J2EE requests reach the thousands and hundreds of thousands levels, then WSAM's machinery must be tuned to accommodate these requests.

This can involve changes at the Data Collector host, on the Managing Server, or both. For WSAM, the most important requirement is to get the monitoring data stowed into its repository. To handle this process at high volumes, WSAM employs queues to house event records until they can be written into the database. Tuning WSAM for J2EE requests with many method calls is mostly a matter of tuning these queues.

Tuning the Managing Server

If there are transmission problems in getting the data from the Data Collector to the Managing Server, or if the problems appear to be localized to the Managing Server itself, then try adjusting these parameters in the psx.properties files:

- cyanea.socket.sendBuffer
  - The default value is 65356. This sets a suggested size for the underlying buffers used by the platform for outgoing network I/O. This is a suggestion from the kernel to the application about the buffer sizes for data to be sent over the socket. Increasing the buffer size can increase the performance of network I/O for high-volume connections; decreasing the size can help to reduce the backlog of incoming data.
- cyanea.socket.recvBuffer
  - The default value is 65356. This sets a suggested size for the underlying buffers used by the platform for incoming network I/O. This is a suggestion from the kernel to the application about the buffer sizes for data to be received over the socket.
- cyanea.ps.aa.maxQueueLength
  - The default value is 10000. This is the maximum queue length between the publish servers and the archive agents. The publish servers buffer events in a queue when the publish server tries to write data to the archive agents faster than the data can be stowed, or if the database or archive agents are down.

Note: This value can be adjusted in WSAM's console too. Go to **Administration → Managing Server → System Properties**. Change the Maximum Method Count as needed.

Tuning the z/OS Data Collector

On the DC side, these two parameters and their defaults affect high-volume processing with large method traces:

- internal.probe.publishing.frequency=2000 (milliseconds)
- internal.probe.event.queue.size.limit=5000

The method record dropping is a feature imposed on the WSAM data collectors to limit the amount of data sent to publishing servers so that controls can be put over the volume and timing of transmitted data. The default setting is more suitable for environments where WSAM MOD (monitor on demand) levels 1 or 2 are in effect. If MOD level 3 is active and the server is under a heavy load, then fine-tune the settings for the Data Collector or the publishing server that is reporting dropped records in their logs.

By default, the Data Collector will send out 5000 records for each application every 2 seconds and will drop all records after the 5000th record. The Data Collector log file reports the number of records dropped versus the total number of records in the queue. This gives system tuners a rough idea about what would be an optimum value for the event queue size. To set the limit to 70000, for example, edit the datacollector.properties file located under <cyanea home>/etc and set:

- internal.probe.event.queue.size.limit=70000

Be aware that changes in the master datacollector.properties file must be propagated to the generated datacollector.properties files (those prefixed with the server name). You must remove the generated datacollector.properties file and the generated gpsCounter.txt file and let the Data Collector regenerate new ones.

Fine-tuning the exclude list in the Data Collector configuration is a good idea too. Identify unwanted Java packages and mark them for exclusion. Method traces with thousands or even millions of method calls are not the best way to monitor systems. Normally, any third-party software packages or products that a customer's application uses ought to be put in the exclude list, unless a problem is suspect with that third-party software.

Each JVM thread has its own queue and is processed every two seconds. Thus, if the application generates more than 5000 records in two seconds of internal processing time, then records will be dropped. Running data collectors at MOD level 3 can create this situation as that can generate hundreds, thousands, sometimes hundreds of thousands or even millions of method entry/exit records.

Also, running single transactions manually and repeatedly means that they are most likely served by the same JVM thread. So, if a request with 1000 method calls is run, it generates 2000 records each time (entry and exit records). Running this request three times consecutively and rapidly overshoots the default 5000 record limit.

CICS and IMS

CSAM and ISAM place a special demand on their host systems. Both products instantiate a JVM within the transaction server's address space (the control region in the case of IMS). The JVM is started under a separate MVS TCB and is used to route monitoring data from the CAM/ISAM monitoring probes in the transaction servers to the WSAM Managing Server. This JVM usually reaches a size of 4 to 5 megabytes (above the line), and room for it must be allotted.

The best way to do this is to change the REGION= parameter on the CICS and IMS jobs to `0M`. This turns off MVS storage limits for the job and allows the address space to acquire the storage needed for the CSAM/ISAM JVM.

If the transaction server already has instantiated JVMs for application processing, then the addition of the CSAM/ISAM JVM should have no impact. Otherwise, make note of the virtual storage requirement mentioned above and also be aware that paging rates may increase if real memory becomes constrained for the transaction server's address spaces.

3.3 Operator procedures and commands

Here are some of the common commands and operator instructions for the WSAM Managing Server.

3.3.1 Starting and stopping the Managing Server's major pieces

The sequence of events when starting up the WSAM Managing Server is very important.

1. Start the virtual frame buffer.
2. Start the database.
3. Start the HTTP Web server (optional).
4. Start the WAS Cyanea server instance (visualization engine).
5. Start the Cyanea components.

If the major pieces are not started in this sequence, then run-time problems can result. For example, how WSAM acquires and controls TCP sockets can be impacted by the Managing Server startup sequence. If the sockets are acquired in the wrong order, then failures with the sockets will be seen in the WAM error logs and processing will be unpredictable.

Starting Xvfb

You will need Virtual Frame Buffer if you are starting WebSphere for the Managing Server from a telnet terminal window. Virtual Frame Buffer is required for the operation of Performance Analysis and Reporting (PAR). If it is not installed, the graphs in PAR will not display.

Linux

To start a virtual X11 environment on Linux, proceed as follows.

To start Xvfb server, enter:

```
$ /usr/bin/nohup /usr/X11R6/bin/Xvfb :1 1>/dev/null 2>/dev/null &
```

AIX

To start the Xvfb server, enter:

```
$ X -vfb -force :1 &
```

or

```
$ /bin/nohup X -vfb -force :1 1>/dev/null 2>/dev/null &
```

With the introduction of the JDK v1.4, there is a built-in feature which provides virtual frame buffering capabilities (graphics display support).

Once virtual frame buffering is activated, the commands for starting up Xvfb can be ignored. Only WSAM v3.1 can use the JDK v1.4.

Starting the repository database

To start DB2 UDB, switch to the userid assigned to the DB2 UDB instance (by default the instance is bd2inst1, and you must know the password for this user):

```
su - db2inst1
```

Then issue the start or stop command:

```
db2start
db2stop
```

Starting the Visualization Engine

To start the visualization engine, switch to root:

su – root (you must know the password)

Start virtual frame buffer. Then issue these commands:

DISPLAY = :1 /opt/WebSphere/AppServer/bin/startupserver.sh server1 &

DISPLAY = :1 /opt/WebSphere/AppServer/bin/startupserver.sh Cyanea &

This will start the WAS server1 instance, which has the admin console. The Cyanea server instance runs the octigate application, which is the WSAM console.

Note: If you followed the instructions in the WSAM V3.1 Installation Guide, then the Cyanea server instance should start automatically when server1 is started.

Starting the HTTP Web server

The HTTP Web server is generally installed when WebSphere Application Server is installed. It is not necessary to use the HTTP Web server, though. The internal HTTP transports of WebSphere can be used instead, both for unprotected data transport and for encrypted data transport using HTTPS protocols.

If you do choose to use an HTTP Web server, WSAM employs the IBM Apache HTTP Web server. It is usually installed into /opt/IBMHttpServer.

To start or stop the HTTP Web server:

su - root

cd /opt/IBMHttpServer/bin

./apachectl start/stop

Starting and stopping the Cyanea components

To start the Cyanea components: enter:

su – cyanea (must know the password)

cd /opt/cyaneaone/bin

sh cyanea-start.sh

To stop the Cyanea components: enter:

su - cyanea (must know the password)

sh cyanea-stop.sh

Note: This will stop all the standalone Java components. It will not stop the WAS Cyanea server instance, nor will it stop the repository database.

3.3.2 General commands for the Cyanea components

The Cyanea components are a Java-based set of processes and servers. Their care and handling requires special attention and control. They are loosely coupled, so it is generally acceptable to bring the components down and up independently of one another.

The Kernel, Publish Server, Archive Agent, Message Dispatcher, Polling Agent, and Global Publish Server are all controlled via a common script "cyaneactl." The syntax is:

`su – cyanea` (must know the password)

./cyaneactl.sh <property file name> <command>

The “property file name” refers to the name of the property file associated with the instance of the component. “Command” refers to one of "start", "stop", "ping", or "status".

Ping and status are health-check commands. Use them to determine whether a component started successfully and is healthy.

The following property files are available by default on the WSAM Managing Server:

- Kl1 - first instance of the kernel
- Kl2 - second instance of the kernel
- ps1 - first instance of the publish server
- ps2 - second instance of the publish server
- sam - the one instance Global Publish Server
- aa1 - first instance of the archive agent
- aa2 - second instance of the archive agent
- md - message dispatcher
- pa - polling agent

To start, stop, ping or check status on the first instance of the kernel, enter:

```
su – cyanea
```

./cyaneactl.sh kl1 start/stop/ping/status

To start, stop, ping, or check status on the second instance, type:

```
./cyaneactl.sh kl2 start
```

To start, stop, ping, or check status on the first instance of the archive agent, enter:

```
su – cyanea
```

./cyaneactl.sh aa1 start/stop/ping/status

To start, stop, ping or check status on the second instance of the archive agent, enter:

su – cyanea

./cyaneactl.sh aa2 start

Watchdog

The Watchdog is a light weight component that manages a particular kernel. If the kernel does not respond, the Watchdog process restarts the kernel. Each kernel has its own Watchdog process. The Watchdog process must be on the machine where the kernel is running.

The Watchdog properties file is named k1wd1.properties. Tune the following properties in the file:

kernelwd.renewal.failure=3

This property takes an integer value. It is the number of times the Watchdog pings the kernel before it restarts the kernel.

kernelwd.ping.interval=5000

This property takes an integer value. Its units are in milliseconds. It is the time between individual pings from the Watchdog to the Kernel.

To start the kernel kl1 with the Watchdog:

cyaneact1.sh kl1 start

To stop the kernel kl1 with the Watchdog:

cyaneactl.sh kl1 stop

To start the kernel kl1 without the Watchdog:

klctl.sh start kl1.properties

To stop the kernel kl1 without the Watchdog:

- klctl.sh stop kl1.properties
- WSAM log maintenance

The following parameters pertain to the log file sizes and the rotations of the log files. The log files are located in <cyanea_home>/etc directory. The log files are:

- log-kl1.properties
- log-kl2.properties
- LogTest.properties
- log-aa.properties
- log-aa1.properties
- log-aa2.properties
- log-am.properties
- log-td.properties
- log-md.properties
- log-ps1.properties
- log-ps2.properties
- log-sam1.properties
- log-ps1.properties
- log-pa.properties

The parameters, which affect the size of the log files and how many log file copies are retained before log wrapping occurs, are:

- MaxFileSize=1000KB
- MaxBackupIndex=10.

4

WSAM V3.1 installation rollout planning

Our objective is to identify generally recommended procedures for rollout planning and more on installation and maintenance for WebSphere Studio Application Monitor Version 3.1.

© Copyright IBM Corp. 2005. All rights reserved.

4.1 Strategic or tactical

The information in this chapter is of a strategic as well as a tactical nature. The rollout planning section is a strategic view to assist in establishing a forward path and direction while the installation and maintenance sections have more of a tactical, "hands on" approach.

4.2 Planning the rollout

WSAM is a sophisticated application itself, much like any application developed for and rolled out to production environments. Rarely are self-developed applications installed into production environments without careful planning and attention to detail, testing procedures, sizing analysis, clearly defined ownership and roles, underlying support mechanisms, and a host of other considerations.

There is an inverse relationship between the time spent planning for a WSAM installation and the time spent performing the installation. For example, at one customer site WSAM was successfully installed into more than 180 production JVMs over the course of three evenings. The key to that success was detailed planning beforehand.

The people involved with WSAM rollout planning and associated support personnel should be familiar with the architecture and components of the WSAM product. A high level diagram of the WSAM architecture identifying the main components and their connectivity is included in Figure 4-1 for reference purposes.

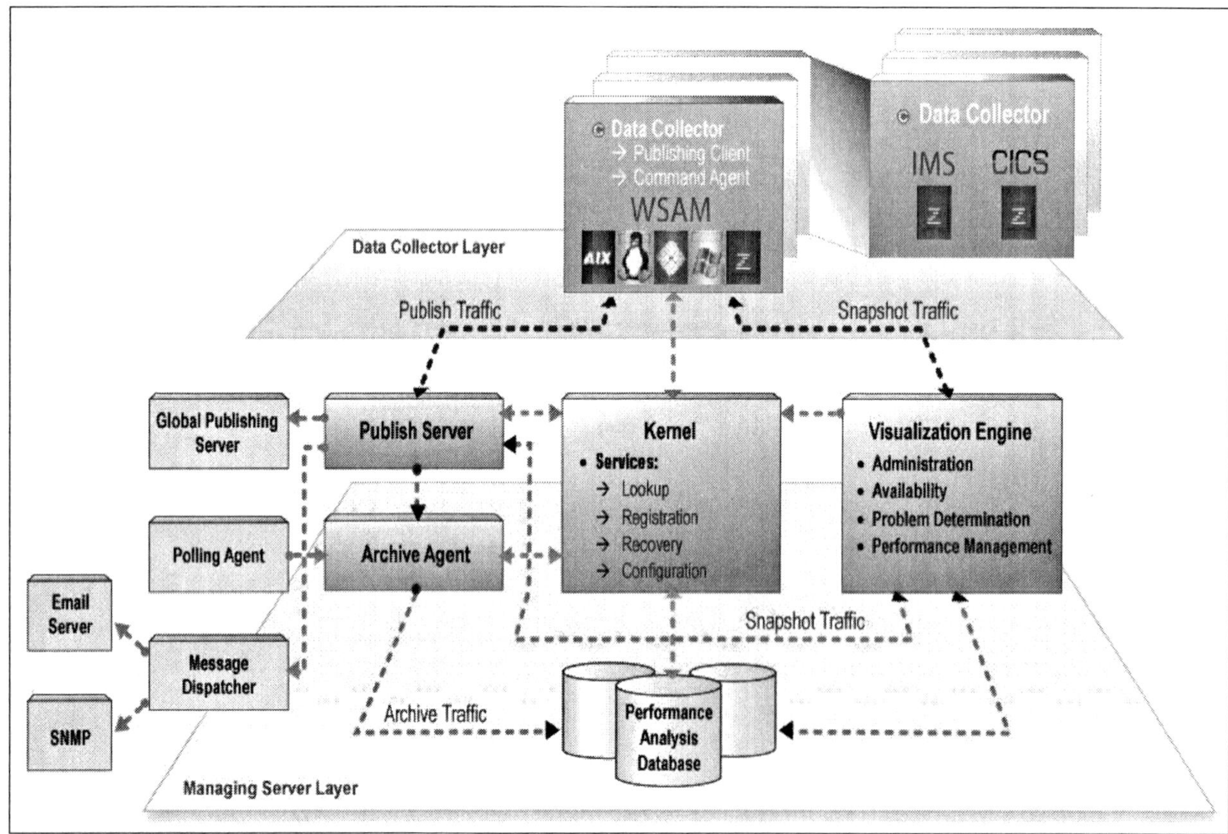

Figure 4-1 WSAM architecture

4.2.1 Identify an enterprise business sponsor and the stakeholders

Sponsors and stakeholders make things happen.

Identify the executive business sponsor

A clearly defined Executive Business sponsor will significantly facilitate implementation. Often the need for support will cross groups as a lower level. Having an executive sponsor often will help if/when you encounter resistance from a group not excited about the opportunity to assist with installation or maintenance.

Define the stakeholders, users, and their requirements

A significant part of the planning effort is to identify WSAM's user community. This usually consists of developers, system administrators, computer operators, and capacity planners. Each group has differing requirements for the type and quantity of data stored, for metrics and reporting, and for any traps and alerts that are generated.

4.2.2 Define ownership

Identify who "owns" WSAM. That is, who will control user access, determine the levels of authorization for users and user groups, decide what data they are permitted to see or act upon, decide how and when product updates will occur, who will apply them, what systems are to be monitored, and at what levels of monitoring? Who will control those decisions, and who will be responsible for collecting sizing data and for ordering Managing Server hardware? In other words, who is the accountable owner of the WSAM product for this installation and who will be providing support within the Customer infrastructure? The roles and people in these roles must be clearly identified.

4.2.3 Choose the project manager

Choose the person and ensure that the individual has adequate resources. Much of the planning work is not technically oriented but requires strong communications, coordination, and organizational skills.

Project managers should familiarize themselves with the sample installation project plan shown in Appendix D, "WSAM sample installation project plan" on page 109.

4.2.4 Educate the user community and gain stakeholder support

Familiarize the user community with WSAM and its benefits; certainly the direct benefits from their unique perspectives. It is much easier to get system administrators to assist in the planning, installation, and testing if they see how the product improves and simplifies their daily jobs. Get as many teams involved as are needed to support the installation.

4.2.5 Identify and document business needs for monitoring

Quantify the reasons you are interested in monitoring and the areas to be monitored. Clarify if it is development, QA, production, or a combination of these. Establish clear and concise goals for monitoring in each of these areas. For example, performance improvement, availability management, problem diagnosis, capacity planning, or combinations of these. Document these goals.

4.2.6 Identify applications and JVMs to monitor

One of the hardest parts of a WSAM installation can be for a company to identify all the Java Virtual Machines (JVMs) they want to monitor. WSAM doesn't monitor specific applications; it monitors all the applications running within a JVM. Identify the applications that you want to monitor and identify the servers on which they run; this is your base for monitoring. As part of installation rollout planning, we suggest a set of spreadsheets to identify Operating Systems, Platform, WebSphere level, and WSAM levels associated with the Managing Server. An example of an identification and timing matrix we have used to identify systems to rollout and time frames is included in Figure 4-2.

WSAM - INVENTORY SYSTEM - PROD.											
Managing Server = WSAMP01					WEBSPHERE				WSAM DC		
	LPAR/SYSTEM	OS	Platform	WAS	Next WAS	Next Date	Current Ver	Date	Next Ver	Patch	Date
Prod	INVENTORYP01	5.1	AIX	5.1.0.2			-	20050201	3.1		
Prod	INVENTORYP02	5.1	AIX	5.1.0.2			-	20050201	3.1		
Prod	INVENTORYP03	5.1	AIX	5.1.0.2			-	20050201	3.1		
Prod	BENEFITP01	11i	HP	5.0.2.2			-	20050201	3.1		
Prod	ACCOUNTSP01	1.4	z/OS	510.202			3.1	20050201			

WSAM - INVENTORY SYSTEM - DEV.											
Managing Server = WSAMD01					WEBSPHERE				WSAM DC		
	LPAR/SYSTEM	OS	Platform	WAS	Next WAS	Next Date	Current Ver	Date	Next Ver	Patch	Date
Dev	INVENTORYD01	5.1	AIX	5.1.0.2			3.1	20041201			
Dev	BENEFITD01	11i	HP	5.0.2.2			3.1	20041215			
Dev	ACCOUNTSD01	1.4	z/OS	510.202			3.1	20041207			

WSAM - CUSTOMER SYSTEM - PROD.											
Managing Server = WSAMP01					WEBSPHERE				WSAM DC		
	LPAR/SYSTEM	OS	Platform	WAS	Next WAS	Next Date	Current Ver	Date	Next Ver	Patch	Date
Prod	CUSTOMERP01	5.1	AIX	5.1.0.2			-	20050115	3.1		
Prod	CUSTOMERP02	5.1	AIX	5.1.0.2			-	20050116	3.1		
Prod	CUSTOMERP03	5.1	AIX	5.1.0.2			-	20050117	3.1		
Prod	CUSTOMERP04	5.1	AIX	5.1.0.2			-	20050118	3.1		

WSAM - CUSTOMER SYSTEM - DEV.											
Managing Server = WSAMD01					WEBSPHERE				WSAM DC		
	LPAR/SYSTEM	OS	Platform	WAS	Next WAS	Next Date	Current Ver	Date	Next Ver	Patch	Date
Dev	CUSTOMERD01	5.1	AIX	5.1.0.2			3.1	20041110			
Dev	CUSTOMERD02	5.1	AIX	5.1.0.2			3.1	20041115			

Figure 4-2 Identified systems and timings matrix

4.2.7 Define appropriate levels of access to the user groups

Now that you have identified the general user community who will have access to the WSAM, begin to break them down into logical work groups. For example:

- WSAM Administrators
- Computer Operator
- Computer Operations Manager
- Developers

- IT Development Managers
- IT Executive Managers
- Capacity Planners
- Report Processors

Each of these groups should probably have different levels of access within WSAM as related to their specific job function. To determine the various levels of access that should be granted to each of the above defined user roles, in the WSAM Administrative console, select:

Administrations → Account Management → Role Configuration

The general categories of authorization or access are Administrations, Availability, Problem Determination, and Performance Management.

Example 1

The Computer Operator group may be granted the ability to "VIEW" all problem determination processes, but only Computer Operations Management may be granted the authority to modify a thread by canceling the thread or changing its priority.

Example 2

The Administrators of WSAM should be granted the ability to alter the WSAM monitoring level and database recording percentage, perhaps the Computer Operations group as well, but not the Developers group.

4.2.8 Define appropriate views to the user groups

As with access rights, groups should probably have differing views of the systems being monitored. Your IT Executive Managers may wish to view only the production systems on their initial landing page when logging onto the WSAM administration console. The Computer Operations Manager may wish to view all systems, development, QA, and production, and see them with a more detailed view of each server. As you define users and groups consider their work interests as you associate the systems they view on their landing page when they log onto the WSAM administrative console.

4.2.9 Plan time frame to implement

The time to install WSAM depends upon the customer's environment and its complexity. Our best practice recommendation is to design for the entire implementation, but initially to implement a limited segment of the production environment for a short period. Once everyone is comfortable with the initial limited rollout, installation onto the remaining environment may be accomplished within a matter of a few days depending upon the size of the environment. This one-step-at-a-time approach permits development of experiential learning not only of the WSAM product, but of any site dependent anomalies if there are any. These site specific considerations may then be used to fine tune the remainder of the rollout process.

4.3 Rollout

The rollout of WSAM has a number of tasks that have to be completed.

4.3.1 Develop WSAM enterprise architecture

Analysis of the WSAM enterprise architecture is a necessary task.

Separation of development and production

Unless there are only a "few" servers (Java Virtual Machines or JVMs), it is usually best to have one Managing Server for Development environments and another for Production environments. The rationale for this recommendation is the traditional one of separating Production and Development systems, as well as considerations about the expected usages of the systems too.

Frequently, there will be servers running at Level 3 (Debugging Mode) and generating much data in a Development environment while in a Production environment the servers will likely be running at Level 1 and generating much less data. Also, the amount of data retained in or archived from the WSAM database will usually be significantly less for a Development environment than for a Production environment.

Managing Servers: Shared versus stand-alone

Our unequivocal recommendation is that the Managing Server be a stand-alone system. When the Managing Server interacts frequently with many Data Collectors, there are significant timing considerations along with network considerations that come into play. Often, computing cycles and memory may be swapped out, thus offering only limited or no compute time. Since the Managing Server communicates with many Data Collectors and monitors "heartbeat" information as well as bi-directional data transfer I/O requests, we have found that a stand-alone system for the Managing Server significantly reduces run-time problems.

Managing Servers: Selection

The Managing Server may be installed on various hardware platforms. Choosing which platform is right for you mostly involves selecting a system which is familiar to your systems programming support teams. The sizing of the Managing Server should be done initially with an IBM IT Architect or IT Specialist familiar with WSAM. They will gather up specific information about your environment to be monitored (see below "database sizing") and then they will provide you with guidance on how many system resources (CPUs, Memory, Disk) are needed to match your planned usage of WSAM.

Resource sizing

In order to size the database, the network load, and recommend a server with appropriate resources to perform the Managing Server functions, the following information will be needed:

- Number of user sessions (users) per day (farm-wide for the JVMs the Managing Server is managing)
- Number of requests per session
- Number of methods per request (identify if average or maximum)
- Total number of JVMs to be monitored
- Number of servers running concurrently at L3
- Garbage collection interval on the JVMs (in seconds)
- Number of days of history to be actively maintained in the database
- WSAM polling interval (optional - default is 60 seconds)
- WSAM sampling rate (optional - default for production is 5%, default for development is 10%)

With the provisioning of this information, your IBM SWITA will be able to utilize a WSAM sizing tool to determine the required configuration as identified in Figure 1-1 on page 4. For example, it will identify the number of Publish Servers, Archive Agents, and Kernels, along with the CPU and Memory requirements for the servers.

An example of how the amount of memory required is determined is from a formula such as:

```
REAL MEMORY = 1 GB for WebSphere & OS
+ 1 GB for DB2 if located on the system
+ [(# PS  * Heapsize)  +  (#AA * Heapsize)  +  (#MD * Heapsize)  +  (# KL * Heapsize)  +
(#GPS * Heapsize)  +  (# PA * Heapsize)  +  (# VE * Heapsize)]
```

This will need to be adjusted for environments utilizing a Managing Server installed across multiple boxes.

Network: Load, port utilization, and firewalls

The same information used to determine database sizing will be used to compute the effective additional load on the network; the load will be calculated in Bits/Second.

The default port utilization is described somewhat implicitly in the WSAM Installation Guide (SC31-6312). Chapter 6, “Firewalls and ports” on page 87 contains an explicit diagram of the Port requirements to implement WSAM, CSAM, and ISAM. There is a WSAM port consolidator that is available on the distributed platforms for WSAM that may reduce the number of ports utilized by WSAM. If the opening of multiple ports either unidirectional or bi-directional are a concern to the installation, this option should be examined.

Firewalls located between the Data Collectors and Managing Server provide an opportunity for problems. Implementation planning must include the local Network Support team. Define and document the Ports that will be needed for WSAM, CSAM, and ISAM; provide this well in advance to your Network team to make sure these ports are opened prior to installation. Chapter 6, “Firewalls and ports” on page 87 provides information regarding firewalls and ports.

High availability and fail over

Are high availability (HA) and fail over (FA) requirements for WSAM? These are subjective calls to be made by the Customer and how they view monitoring. For some, having a monitor unavailable due to a hardware (system, disk, or network) failure for several hours may be a non-issue. For other companies, they may view running in production without monitoring similar to driving at night without headlights. Once you have decided how your company views monitoring, then work with one of your WSAM IT Architects or Services personnel to provide a set of options. The Managing Server can run as a single server with WebSphere/WebLogic installed along with the relational database. This can also be spread across two or more boxes and a SAN to provide a most robust HA and FO architecture.

Large scale installations

For installations planning to monitor large numbers of Data Collectors, the topography of the Managing Server components should be adjusted to accommodate the workload. This will include defining additional Archive Agents, Publishing Servers, adjusting Managing Server internal startup scripts to accommodate the additional components and changes to Managing Server tuning parameters. For documentation purposes, we define "Large Scale" as one Managing Server supporting 50 or more Data Collectors. We are currently developing detailed documentation to address "Large Scale Installations"; contact your IBM Account Representative for access to this documentation as it becomes available.

The number of dedicated ports required by WSAM for a default installation may be an issue for larger environments. Consider utilization of the Port Consolidator tool available (on distributed WSAM Data Collectors) to significantly reduce the number of ports required. At the time of writing this IBM Redbook, the z/OS version of the port consolidator is not yet available; the plan is for this to become available in the not too distant future.

Appendix C, “Multi-Box Managing Server installation” on page 103, contains information regarding installation of a Managing Server on multiple systems.

Security considerations

Security and associated considerations need to be an integrated component of planning for any implementation. WSAM has adopted the approach to try and utilize the underlying security infrastructure of the Operating System upon which it is installed when possible. For the Managing Server, users that are defined to access the WSAM administrative console must be defined or associated with users defined on the base Operating System. WebSphere Global Security and J2EE security are supported. When installing WSAM into a Data Collector environment with J2EE security implemented, be sure to modify the local security policy to provide access for WebSphere to the appropriate newly defined WSAM libraries.

WSAM does not explicitly perform encryption of the database.

Node authentication is an option that is available with WSAM. Appendix B, “Security: Node authentication” on page 97, provides a more detailed description of how Node authentication may be implemented in WSAM.

4.4 Establish a training plan

Setup training schedules. We have found there are four general groups who should become familiar with the product.

- Management - They should have a simple overview of the product, identifying how it may benefit their team. This will help when it comes time to have members of their team participate in a usage training session.
- Administrators - The team that will be providing administrative support of WSAM should have a session on adding users, maintenance, and trap enablement as well as usage. Often they will be viewed as the Subject Matter Experts on the product.
- Operations - A training session for operations is usually a four hour window to demonstrate how the product can assist them in fast production problem resolution.
- Developers - Often this is best broken down into two sessions with a one or two week interval between. The initial training may be one half to one full day. Once the developers have started using the products they will become more advanced and will have developed deep questions on how to either interpret values or how to better resolve their specific problems. This can be covered in a follow up advanced training session.

When planning for training, consider two sets of training sessions. An initial session which will provide the basic training followed up one to four weeks later with a more advanced training agenda of one day. As with any product, once the user community starts working with the product, their sophistication level will increase and they will generate questions that would not be best covered in an initial training session. This would include advanced data analysis and perhaps more advanced settings of traps as well as potential SNMP interfaces enablement to other "system" type monitors such as the Tivoli Tec console.

4.5 Identify reporting requirements

Determine who will be interested in the reports available from WSAM. IT senior management usually prefer summarized reports. With WSAM, they also get reports that are platform agnostic; WSAM supports a variety of mainframe and distributed environments (Linux for zSeries, Intel, HP/UX, Solaris, Windows, AIX, z/OS, and WebLogic). Operations personnel and Capacity Planners may want periodic reports to check on usage and service level commitments. While WSAM V3.1 permits scheduling reports to facilitate reporting on a given schedule, some Customer requirements may be more sophisticated. In addition to the built-in reports, monitoring data is stored in a standard relational database; this permits the development of local SQL-based reports for customers' specific criteria. Third party report generators may be used to build custom reports. Contact your IBM representative to request a copy of the database schema associated with your version of WSAM.

4.6 Identify implementation team

Do you wish to dedicate your resources to the planning and experiential learning that comes with an installation or is it more cost-effective to bring in a Subject Matter Expert? Our Best Practice recommendation is to consider utilizing Professional Services to do the initial rollout, train the Project Manager, and shorten their learning curve. Judicious use of Services will provide a fast-track hands-on initial learning experience for the customer WSAM support team who may then continue the rollout with their newly developed WSAM rollout skills. Overall, you should commit to self-sufficiency.

4.7 Identify initial deployment benefits

As stated earlier in the "Plan time frame to implement" section above, we recommend an initial installation on a small scale. Use this initial implementation to identify any immediate benefits from the product and share these successes within the organization. This may help with internal support as the rollout continues.

4.8 Installation

This paper augments the *WSAM V3.1 Installation Guide* with our experiences and recommendations for installing WSAM V3.1.

4.8.1 Before you start

Before you begin implementing WSAM V3.1, make sure you have all the necessary resources available, including trained and organized teams to implement the installation.

A successful installation of WSAM V3.1 requires careful planning and education. It also requires good understanding of the WebSphere J2EE Application Servers, and a working knowledge of relational database and operating system maintenance procedures.

4.8.2 Planning the installation

Analysis of the environment for installation is critical.

Review the initial needs for the installation

These questions should be answered before setting up WSAM:

- Do you have to coordinate availability of the systems with representatives from other teams?
- Do you have access to all the necessary resources?
- Is there any network, database, or server maintenance already scheduled which might interrupt the installation process?
- Are there any firewall issues which might prevent communication between Data Collector and Managing Server?
- Are there any security, network connectivity, availability, and performance issues that you need to consider during this project?

Product Implementation checklist

Gather environment related data:

  - Study the existing application servers' topology.
  - identify where WSAM DCs are to be installed on all servers.
  - Identify the machine where the WSAM MS is to be installed.
  - Get the O/S type and version, Database type and version, and Application Server type and version.
  - Make sure that all hardware and software is supported.
  - Find out if there is a firewall between any DC and MS machines. If so, make sure the ports for communications between Managing Server and Data Collector are opened in the firewall.
  - Find out if you have earlier versions of WSAM on any of the targeted servers. If so, decide whether you want to upgrade WSAM or if you want to install WSAM as a new product.

- Size up the resources.
  - Make sure that the hardware resources selected for DC and MS installations meet the prerequisites for WSAM Installation.

- Based on expected volume, decide if you need to install various MS components on different machines.

- Gather all the inputs required for DC Installation.
  - The inputs are listed in the sample input file provided in WSAM installer.
  - The sample input file dcInputs_Sample.txt is located in Installer-DC/etc. directory.
- Gather following inputs required for MS Installation.
  - The inputs are listed in sample input file provided in WSAM installer.
  - The sample input file msInputs_Sample.txt is located in Installer-MS/etc directory.

Know where the most valuable resources are and how to get them.

- Publications
  - Installation guide, operator's guide and other publications are provided on the WSAM CD.
  - Installation training material can be obtained from the IBM WSAM Services team.
- Download Web site
  - Make sure you have access to download site, if you do not already have a product CD.
- IBM Redbooks
  - You can search for, view, or download IBM Redbooks, Redpapers, Hints and Tips, draft publications and additional materials, as well as order hardcopy IBM Redbooks or CD-ROMs, at this Web site:

    `http://www.ibm.com/redbooks`

Identify the team with various skill sets

- Identify the Unix Administrator, if you do not have "root" user permission for the Server where MS is going to be installed.
- Identify Database Administrator, in case you need any database-related help during MS installation.
- Identify the Application Server (WebSphere) Administrator, in case you need any help with WebSphere or WebLogic.
- For z/OS installations, you need to include a Systems Programmer and RACF® support person. If you are installing a CICS and IMS Data Collector, a Systems Support person for each subsystem will also need to be involved.

4.8.3 Installing WSAM

Make sure you have the installation guide handy and follow the instructions carefully. It is very important to follow the steps in the installation guide very carefully. Spending a few more minutes to read every step during installation is completely worth it, as it takes hours to debug a problem if you skip or misread a step during installation.

Familiarize yourself with various scripts provided by installer. Installer design training material describes various scripts and their usage.

If you are installing in just one box, we recommend interactive installer. But if you are going to install WSAM in a server farm, we recommend silent installer.

If you are using silent installer, make sure you read and follow instructions before each input line very carefully. Since silent installer is not interactive, you may not be able to find the problem until the installation is complete and you check the log files.

Any problems or errors that occur during installation are communicated to the user via log files, and they are not printed in console. Always check the log files after installation. Make sure there are no error messages in the log files. Also make sure all the files are installed and Application Servers are configured.

4.8.4 Major Tasks performed by the installer

Following are the major tasks performed by Data Collector and Managing Server installers.

Major tasks performed by Data Collector installer

Complete a prerequisite check. Verify that the prerequisites are met for installing Data Collector. You may force installation, even if prerequisites are not met, using "-force" option.

Install files

This component copies Data Collector-related files, and modifies the necessary files for Data Collector installation. The bill of materials file - "bom.dc" contains the list of files to be copied.

Configure application server

One of the major tasks of installation is applying configuration to each application server where Data Collector is being installed. Configuration varies for various combinations of o/s, application server, and version of application server. For flexibility, the configuration templates are stored as XML files.

Major tasks performed by the Managing Server installer

Complete a prerequisite check. This component verifies that the prerequisites are met for installing Managing Server. You may force installation, even if prerequisites are not met, using "-force" option.

Install files

This component copies Managing Server-related files, and modifies the necessary files for Managing Server installation. The bill of materials file - "bom.ms" contains the list of files to be copied.

Install visualization engine

One of the major tasks of installation is installing visualization engine. A new application server is created (we will call it "cyanea" server), and used for installing visualization engine. If a server with the same name exists, it is deleted and recreated. After creating a new server cyanea, octigate.ear is deployed on cyanea server. Necessary configuration changes are applied to the cyanea server.

Create local database

Another major task completed by installer is optional creation of local database. DB2 or Oracle can be used for Managing Server.

4.8.5 Installation scripts

Installer includes many shell/batch scripts, which can be used for various installation tasks. These scripts can be used directly for performing a particular installation-related task.

Data Collector installation scripts

Next we cover the Data Collector installation scripts.

install-DC.sh

This is the main script for installation. User starts installation by running this script.

prereq.sh

This script verifies the prerequisites prior to starting installation. This script can be used directly to check if the prerequisites are met or not.

install-configure.sh

This script installs files and configures application server. It invokes installFiles.sh, genConcreteConfig.sh, and applyConfig.sh in this sequence.

install-only.sh

This script installs Data Collector-related files. Configuration will be skipped. It invokes installFiles.sh.

installFiles.sh

This script is used for copying and modifying files.

genConcreteConfig.sh

This script is used for generating concrete configuration files from XML-formatted template.

applyConfig.sh

This script is used for applying configuration. genConcreConfig.sh has to be run before running this script.

Managing Server installation scripts

Next we cover the Managing Server installation scripts.

install-MS.sh

This is the main script for installation. User starts installation by running this script. It invokes prereq.sh and install-configure.sh

prereq.sh

This script verifies the prerequisites prior to starting installation. This script can be used directly to check if the prerequisites are met or not.

install-configure.sh

This script installs files and configures application server. It invokes installFiles.sh, ManagingDevice.sh, and Database.sh in this sequence.

installFiles.sh

This script is used for installing files.

ManagingDevice.sh

This script is used for installing Managing Server. It uses WS_Install_VE.jacl or WL_InstallVE.sh for installing visualization engine. It also uses WS_DB2_JDBC_DRIVER.jacl and WS_DB2_ORACLE_DRIVER.jacl for setting up database driver.

4.8.6 Common mistakes

The most common mistakes made during installation are:

- Not entering fully qualified node name and server names while using silent installer.
- Not using correct user while starting Managing Server, Database , or WebSphere.
- Not sourcing DB2 profile, when necessary.
- Entering incorrect inputs during installation.
- Not providing user id / password, when global security is on.
- Trying to use Managing Server when database server is not running.
- Ports not being open in firewall between Managing Server and Data Collector machines.
- Providing incorrect Managing Server IP and/or port during Data Collector installation.
- Not providing fully-qualified Managing Server hostname while installing Data Collector.
- Leaving trailing blank spaces in input file while silent installer for Windows causes a problem.

4.8.7 Resolving installation issues

For the most common installation issues, the following procedures should be followed.

- Familiarize yourself with various log files for various tasks performed by installer.
- Check the log files to find out the exact cause of problem.
- To find out if a file has not been copied, check installFiles.log file. It is very likely that the patch level of Application Server has not matched while copying file.
- If configuration has not been applied to one or more of the servers, check configuration.log file. Also check if generated concrete configuration XML files (cfg_aix_was_51_server1_Gen.xml) are there in cyanea_installer_dc or cyanea_installer_ms directories. If the generated files are missing, you may use "genConcreteConfig.sh" script to generate the configuration files, and then use "applyConfig.sh" to apply the configuration.
- If Data Collector does not come up after installation, check the application server log files for the server where Data Collector has been installed.
- If Managing Server does not come up, check the log files for Managing Server. Also make sure, the database is up and running.
- If Data Collector and Managing Server both are up and running, but Data Collector does not show up in configuration list in Visualization Engine, check the host, port of Managing Server in datacollector.properties and datacollector.policy files.
- If Managing Server comes up, but you get "Please contact your System Administrator" while trying to log in, check the MS server hostname / IP address, port in bin/setenv.sh, and in various properties file in "etc" directory. Also, check the log files to see any error messages.

4.8.8 Installation log files

Always check the installation log files.

- For debugging any issue related to installer, please check the log files.
- There are various log files for different tasks performed by installer.

Data Collector installation logs

Data collector installation log files are as follows:

- installer-dc.log is an overall log file which summarizes all the tasks.
- prereqCheck.log will show if system met prerequisites or not.
- installFiles-dc.log will contain information about copying files. Make sure there are no failed file copy operations.
- configuration.log contains information about applying configuration.
- User inputs file dcInputs.txt, which is located in logs directory, contains all the user inputs used during installation. It is helpful in verifying that all the inputs were correct.

Managing Server installation logs

Managing Server installation logs are as follows:

- installer-ms.log is an overall log file which summarizes all the tasks.
- prereqCheck.log will show if the system met prerequisites or not.
- installFiles-ms.log will contain information about copying files. Make sure there are no failed file copy operations.
- managingDevice.out and managingDevice.err contain information about installing the Managing Server.
- User inputs file msInputs.txt, which is located in logs directory, contains all the user inputs used during installation. It is helpful in verifying that all the inputs were correct.

4.9 Platform specific issues

Next we cover a number of platform specific issues.

4.9.1 Customized startup and shutdown instructions

All the information required to start and stop the WSAM Managing Server is located within the Installation and Customization Guide. If there is a server problem and the Managing Server needs to be shutdown or restarted, trying to locate the instructions in a manual is not convenient. Create a set of customized, installation specific instructions to be inserted into a "run-book" that will be handy for the administrator managing WSAM. An example of such a startup and shutdown sheet is located in Figure 4-3 on page 62 and Figure 4-4 on page 63. Be sure to adjust this example to your specific installation requirements.

With the implementation of JDK 1.4.x there is a new property that removes the need for starting a new Xserver with Virtual Frame Buffer support to provide the graphical environment we need on the Managing Server for WSAM. The variable is java.awt.headless=true. In the WebSphere Administration Console go to **Application Servers** → **Cyanea** → **Process Definition** → **Java Virtual Machine** and create this as a new property with the value of "true" and then recycle the server.

WSAM STARTUP PROCEDURES

Please follow these instructions, in this order when restarting the WSAM managing server from a reboot. Commands listed below are in quotes (""), when you do it on the machine, please leave out the quotes! These instructions presume that you have installed the WSAM components in it's defaults locations.

1)Open a new Telnet window and perform the following in this one Telnet session.

2)Log onto the Managing Server system as root

3)STOP DB2: Type: "su - db2inst1" (become the DB2 admin user)

4)RESTART DB2: Type: "db2stop" and when you have your prompt back, type: "db2start" (we're making sure here that the DB started properly)

5)Type: "ps -ef | grep db2" (you should see a bunch of DB2 processes running)

6)Type: "exit" (so you should be root again), you can check this by typing: "id" to see who you are logged in as

7)Start the virtual framebuffer:
Linux:
Then type: "/usr/X11R6/bin/Xvfb :1 -auth /root/.Xauthority -screen 0 1024x768x8 &"
AIX:
Type: "nohup X -vfb -force :1 &"
Type: DISPLAY=<ip of managing server>:1 ; export DISPLAY
Type: env | grep DISPLAY

8)START WEBSPHERE: Type: "cd /opt/WebSphere/AppServer/bin" (or change to the bin directory of your WebSphere installation)

9)Type: "./startupServer.sh &" and then type: "tail -f ../logs/tracefile" (watch the logfile, make sure there are no exceptions/errors and that you see the message: Server __adminServer open for e-business). Once you have confirmed this, you can type: "Ctrl c" (hold down the Ctrl key and type c to get your prompt back).

10) If you are working from a workstation and wish to view the WebSphere Administration Console Type: export DISPLAY=<workstation ip>:0

11) START WSAM: Then change user to cyanea (su - cyanea) and type: "cd /opt/cyaneaone/bin" (or change to the bin directory of your cyaneaone installation)

12) Type: "./cyanea-start.sh &" (you should see a bunch of message saying 'Successfully joined Kernel') after the "SAMGPS" messages you can hit enter to get your prompt back.

13) START HTTPSERVER: Type "exit" to become root, or "su - root" and start the HTTP server by typing: "/opt/IBMHTTPServer/bin/apachectl start"

Figure 4-3 WSAM startup procedures

WSAM SHUTDOWN PROCEDURES

1)Shutdown WSAM as the cyanea user: "su - cyanea" then "cd /opt/cyaneaone/bin" and type "./cyanea-stop.sh" This will take a few minutes to stop. You can check to make sure it has finished by typing the command: "ps -ef | grep cyanea", you shouldn't see anymore java processes owned by the cyanea user. If for some reason the processes do not die, you will need to kill it by hand with a "kill -9 PID" where PID is the actual java process id.

2)Shutdown WebSphere. You will need to be root to do this, so type "exit" or "su - root". On a Linux system you can issue the following command: "killall java" on a AIX machine you need to do a "ps -ef | grep java" and "kill -9 PID" (where PID is the process id of the java processes). Check to make sure all of the java processes are gone by typing: "ps -ef | grep java". On occasion these threads won't die right away, so you might need to run the above commands a few times.

3)Shutdown DB2. This can only be done after WebSphere is shutdown. First become the db2 admin user: "su - db2inst1" then type "db2stop". Verify that it has stopped by typing: "ps -ef | grep db2"

4)Type "exit" to become root again or "su - root" and stop the http server as follow: /opt/IBMHTTPServer/bin/apachectl stop"

5)If you need to kill Xvfb type: "ps -ef | grep Xvfb" and "kill -9 PID" where PID is the process id of the Xvfb command.

Figure 4-4 WSAM shutdown procedures

z/OS CICS considerations

Please refer to the IBM Redbook *Installing WebSphere Studio Application Monitor Version 3.1,* SG24-6491-00, Chapter titled The z/OS CICS/TS Data Collector.

z/OS IMS considerations

Please refer to the IBM Redbook *Installing WebSphere Studio Application Monitor Version 3.1,* SG24-6491-00, Chapter titled The z/OS IMS Data Collector.

z/OS WSAM considerations

Please refer to the IBM Redbook *Installing WebSphere Studio Application Monitor Version 3.1,* SG24-6491-00, Chapter titled The Data Collector for z/OS.

4.9.2 Common error messages and solutions

For Managing Server installation

In regard to the Managing Server installation, common error messages and solutions are as follows:

- Installer cannot connect to the server:
  - Please verify that the hostname and port numbers are correct, and the server/deployment manager is up.
- Installer did not copy some of the files:
  - Either the file is missing in the source, or the rule for copying file did not match. If file exists, it can be copied manually.

- Installer's first panel does not show up:
  - If you are installing remotely, make sure that the display has been exported correctly. If you are installing locally, make sure your system is capable of graphical display.
- Getting "SQL Unsatisfied link error" when starting cyanea server after installation:
  - It means db2 profile was not sourced before starting WebSphere or MS.
- DC is not joining MS:
  - Make sure the IP address/host name of MS in DC is correct.
- Socket Exception: connection refused
  - Check setenv.sh for host and port numbers for various MS components.
  - Try "db2 connect to octigate"
  - Try "aactl.sh dbtest"
  - Check kernel log to see if all the components are started or not.
- If you see following exception:
  - Trying to execute prepared statement on connection
  - Exception in thread "main" COM.ibm.db2.jdbc.DB2Exception: [IBM][CLI Driver][DB2/LINUX] SQL0204N "DB2INST1.PROBES" is an undefined name. SQLSTATE=42704
    - That means the user who ran DB scripts (cyaneaone.sql) and the user who is starting MS are not same. Check../bin/setenv.sh for DB user. If it is missing, MS will use default user.
- When DC is not showing up in VE's configuration list:
  - The following SQL statement can be used to find out if DC is in MS database or not.
    - DB2 "select * from servers where controllerid='...id in the MS log fil'"."'
- If there is a problem with RMI connection, and DC cannot join kernel, the host name / port number is not right, you may get following exception: com.cyanea.kernel.core.KernelRMIImpl.CYNK0091E java.lang.reflect.InvocationTargetException
  - In this case, if it is too hard to figure out which property/configuration file has the wrong host, adding the following system property, and restarting DC will fix the problem.

    "java.rmi.server.hostname=DC ip address"
  - Note that this property is not necessary if everything goes right during installation. It is just a work around.
- Getting DB2 exception: "not enough log space"
  - Increase space in DB2 instance log space location. (for example, /home/db2inst1)
  - You may find out log space location by using "db2 get dbconfig"

For Data Collector installation

In regard to the Data Collector installation, common error messages and solutions are as follows:

- Installer cannot connect to the server:
  - Please verify that the hostname and port numbers are correct, and the server/deployment manager is up.

- Installer did not apply configuration:
  - Check that concrete configuration file was generated for each server.
- Installer did not copy some files:
  - Either the file is missing in the source, or the rule for copying file did not match. If file exists, it can be copied manually.
- Installer's first panel does not show up:
  - If you are installing remotely, make sure that the display has been exported correctly. If you are installing locally, make sure your system is capable of graphical display.
- Data Collector did not join Kernel after installation:
  - Make sure the kernel hostname and port number that you entered are correct, the kernel is up, and the necessary host/ports are open between Data Collector and kernel.
- Configuration did not apply and you get wsadmin script errors:
  - Make sure all the necessary variables are replaced while generating concrete configuration files. Search for "@{" string in generated configuration XML files.

4.10 Maintenance

Next we cover maintenance-related tasks and recommendations.

4.10.1 Assign responsibilities

Have a designated WSAM Administrator to take care of WSAM-related issues. Restrict the access for various users based on various roles for using and changing the configuration of WSAM components.

4.10.2 Training

Sending your WSAM administrator and WSAM users to training will be very helpful in fully utilizing WSAM capabilities. Advanced training provides in-depth knowledge of WSAM advanced usage for solving various performance-related problems.

4.11 Database maintenance

Use Data Trimmer to trim unnecessary data. Data trimmer usage information is provided in the user guide that is shipped with WSAM. If you need to move the database server from one machine to another or if you need to migrate from an old version of WSAM to a newer version, you may use data migration scripts to migrate data. The usage information is provided in the user guide that is shipped with WSAM.

Make sure the database has enough log space. Deletion of large amounts of data versus smaller, more frequent deletions can "chew up" the log space quickly. Work with your DBA to determine the appropriate amount of log space for your installation.

In the rollout planning section, you identified how many days of data you wish to keep in the database. Once you start using WSAM you may find it more convenient, especially if use expands beyond your initial estimates, to store reports generated from WSAM and remove the raw data from the database. You have the ability to store reports within WSAM, export reports into PDF files, or store them in other format external data files.

Involve your DBA to maintain the database. Ask the DBA to establish a daily automated job to monitor the database and trigger an e-mail to the WSAM owner if the database uses more than 70% of the available space. Also, ask the DBA to monitor the database with a periodic RUNSTAT, and REORG the database at least weekly and at off-peak-load hours.

Refer to Appendix A, "Database setting information" on page 95 for a more detailed description of how best to tune the WSAM database.

4.12 Monitoring

Make sure you are not gathering data about too many unnecessary classes or packages. It can be modified using Visualization Engine on Data Collector configuration page. Intercepting too many classes may put a heavy load on the database and the server.

Make sure your sampling rate is reasonable. Setting your sampling rate to 100% helps pinpoint a specific problem, but it puts a heavy load on the server. The default sampling rate is 2%. If you have changed it to a very high number to pinpoint a problem, make sure you change it back to a reasonable value.

A higher monitoring level (L3) provides more details for tuning performance and debugging a problem. But, it also has a big overhead. It is not recommended to keep the monitoring level to L3 all the time. You may set it to L3 while debugging a specific problem, and set it back to L1 or L2 level, once debugging is finished.

Always check the log files for any warning or error messages. It will help prevent or debug many problems related to WSAM.

4.13 Upgrade maintenance strategy

The following are recommendations for an upgrade maintenance strategy.

4.13.1 Pre-production testing

As with any software installation, testing in a pre-production environment is *highly* recommended. This permits localized experiential learning associated with any unique Customer environmental issues that could appear as a software conflict. While such problems are not expected, software is what it is.

4.13.2 Software upgrades

Identify when new versions of the Operating System, WebSphere, and WSAM are available. In some cases, these need to be coordinated, depending upon co- and prerequisites for each product. Determine if there are any considerations on upgrading the Managing Server that might have an impact on those Data Collectors that will not be upgraded.

4.13.3 Updating a large number of servers (Data Collectors)

When updating a large number of Servers with new versions of WebSphere and or WSAM, consider utilizing a script that is custom developed for your unique environment.

5

Troubleshooting

The Managing Server's Cyanea overseer components run in background or “silent” mode. WSAM's data collectors always run silently or in background mode inside the monitored systems, too. As with any software environment, though, problems can arise either when installing and configuring the product, or when running and using it.

Since WSAM typically runs silently, most of its diagnostic information is written to sequential log files, either WSAM-owned logs or logs owned by other products and systems. This chapter offers suggestions about debugging methods, tools, techniques, and where the pertinent information for troubleshooting resides.

© Copyright IBM Corp. 2005. All rights reserved.

5.1 General Instructions

There are typical procedures to be followed whenever problems crop up with WSAM. As with any sophisticated software product, most of these steps employ methods, practices, and routines commonly used by systems programmers. These steps are:

- Take note of the failure's characteristics, including the exact time when the problem occurred.
- Try to render an accurate, concise description of the surface symptoms.
- Look for errors in the failing system's joblog and in the application server's std.out and error.out logs.
- Review the error codes in the Messages and Codes manuals for WebSphere and WSAM.
- Look for errors in the failing component's Data Collector log.
- Review the configuration files in the failing component's /etc directory.
- Examine the Managing Server's logs, especially the kernel (kl), archive agent (aa), and publish server (ps) logs, at the same date and time when the failures occurred. Work backwards for some ways to identify any contributing or related anomalies.
- Examine any WSAM Managing Server overseer component logs if necessary.
- Review the troubleshooting best practices documents and FAQs on the IBM WSAM Web site periodically.
- If no resolution is reached at this point, then follow IBM standard practices for Level 1 and Level 2 problem reporting and determination.

Note: One of the most important things to realize early on in working with WSAM is that errors reported in one place, perhaps on a z/OS WebSphere Data Collector, may in fact be caused by problems happening elsewhere.

For example, when a monitored WebSphere J2EE servant address space initializes, the Managing Server passes either its host DNS name or IP address to the remote Data Collector. The Data Collector then opens an RMI connection to the Managing Server to download a copy of the Java class ppe.publish.pe. If this download operation fails, the z/OS WebSphere WSAM datacollector.log reports the failure as a Java class-not-found exception.

That does not mean, as might reasonably be expected, that the class is missing from a JAR file somewhere on the z/OS LPAR. Rather, the problem is usually caused by failures when opening RMI connections successfully from the Data Collector on z/OS to the Managing Server. The fix for this problem is to change the Managing Server's configuration files so that its DNS name or IP address, whichever works, is passed to the Data Collector.

So, a problem reported by the z/OS WebSphere WSAM Data Collector as a Java class exception is really a problem with configuration files on the Managing Server, and you must go there to fix it.

Another problem that arises frequently is when the WSAM console is displaying data as expected and then suddenly data reporting stops. All the throughput volumes and response times graphs on the console's default landing page stop showing any data. Data about throughput volumes and response times is saved in the WSAM repository and retrieved from there for display in the console. Therefore, if a problem like this occurs, there are a couple of possibilities:

- If data is being presented for some servers but not others, then check whether the servers showing no data are running, or have they ended?

- If there is no data for any server in the console, then check whether monitoring traffic is in fact flowing between the data collectors and the Managing Server. Network problems could be hampering the delivery of data to the Managing Server.
- If data is flowing across the connections, then check whether there are problems with the WSAM repository. The relational database may be full, a tablespace might be filled, or indexes might have become corrupted. Any of the problems that can crop up with relational databases can affect WSAM, too. The health of the relational database is very important to WSAM.

5.2 The Managing Server

Many problems that manifest themselves on remote components in WSAM are really caused by problems on the Managing Server. Some knowledge about the operational facilities and the debugging tools available on the Managing Server is essential.

5.2.1 Managing Server self-diagnosis

In the WSAM console under the Administration tab is a self-diagnosis option. This feature takes you to a series of panels that show the status of the Managing Server itself. The health of the Cyanea overseer components and their connections to one another is displayed real-time. See the *WSAM V3.1 User's Guide* for more information about the self-diagnosis panels and the data on them.

5.2.2 Managing Server recovery procedures

These procedures are useful when starting up the WSAM Managing Server after a reboot, and when shutting down the Managing Server.

Starting up the Managing Server

Please follow these instructions when recovering the WSAM Managing Server from a reboot. The commands listed below are in quotes (""), when you execute them on a machine, leave out the quotes. These instructions presume that all WSAM parts are installed into their default locations:

- Log in as root.
- Start the virtual frame buffer:
  - for Linux:
    - Type: "/usr/X11R6/bin/Xvfb :1 -auth /root/.Xauthority -screen 0 1024x768x8 &"
  - for AIX:
    - Type: "X -vfb -force :1 &"
- Start the database:
  - Type: "su - db2inst1" (become the DB2 admin user).
  - Type: "db2stop"
  - When you have your prompt back, type: "db2start". (We are making sure here that the database started properly.)
  - Type: "ps -ef I grep db2" (you should see some DB2 processes running).
- Type: "exit" (so you should be root again. If not, type "su- root"; you can check this by typing: "id" to see who you are logged in as)

- Start the HTTP server:
  - "/opt/IBMHTTPServer/bin/apachectl start"
- Start WebSphere:
  - Type: "cd /opt/WebSphere/AppServer/bin" (or change to the bin directory of your WebSphere installation)
  - Type: "./startServer.sh &" and then type: "tail -f ../logs/tracefile" (watch the logfile, make sure there are no exceptions or errors and that you see the message: Server __adminServer open for e-business). Once you have confirmed this, you can type: "Ctrl c" (hold down the Ctrl key and type c to get your prompt back).
- Start up the Cyanea overseer components.
  - Then change user to cyanea (su - cyanea) and type: "cd /opt/cyaneaone/bin" (or change to the bin directory of your cyaneaone installation).
  - Type: "./cyanea-start.sh &" (you should see a bunch of messages saying "Successfully joined Kernel") after the "SAMGPS" message, you can Press Enter to get your prompt back.

Shutting down the Managing Server

- First shut down the Cyanea overseer components. Login as the cyanea user: "su - cyanea", then type the commands:
  - cd /opt/cyaneaone/bin
  - ./cyanea-stop.sh
- This will take a few minutes to stop. Check to make sure it is finished by typing the command: "ps -ef I grep cyanea", the processes do not die, you must kill them manually:
  - kill -9 PID (where PID is the Java process id).
- Next shut down WebSphere:
  - You will need to be root to do this, so type "exit" or "su - root".
  - Type: "cd /opt/WebSphere/AppServer/bin" (or change to the bin directory of your WebSphere installation.)
  - Type: "./stopServer.sh &" and then type: "tail -f ../logs/tracefile" (watch the logfile, make sure there are no exceptions or errors. Once you have confirmed this, you can type: "Ctrl c" (hold down the Ctrl key and type c to get your prompt back).
  - On a Linux system, you can issue the following command: "killall java"; on a AIX machine, you need to do a "ps -ef I grep java" and "kill -9 PID" (where PID is the process id of the Java processes). Check to make sure all of the Java processes are gone by typing: "ps -ef I grep java". On occasion, these threads won't die right away, so you might need to run the above commands a few times.
- Stop the HTTP Web server as follows:
  - /opt/IBMHTTPServer/bin/apachectl stop
- Then restart the database. This can only be done after WebSphere is shutdown.
  - First become the db2 admin user: "su - db2inst1"
  - then type "db2stop".
  - Verify that it has stopped by typing: "ps -ef I grep db2"
- Type: "exit" (so you should be root again. If not, type "su- root"; you can check this by typing: "id" to see who you are logged in as).
- If you need to, kill Xvfb:

- ps -ef | grep Xvfb
- kill -9 PID (where PID is the process id of the Xvfb command).

5.2.3 Managing Server logs

The Managing Server's Cyanea overseer components operate in background or "silent" mode. Consequently, information about their activities is recorded in sequential log files. The log files, which are typically found at /opt/cyaneaone/logs, are the primary source of information about the Managing Server itself.

The kl (kernel), aa (archive agent), and ps (publish server) logs are the most important ones for most problems. They show the status of connection and configuration attempts between the Managing Server and its data collectors, the status of traffic flowing from the data collectors to the Managing Server, and the status of attempts to store the monitoring data into the WSAM repository.

If request correlation monitoring is to be engaged at your site, then the sam log is important too. It shows whether WSAM was successful in associating different pieces of processing together into a composite request view.

5.3 The Data Collectors

Most of WSAM operates in a background mode. This includes the Managing Server's overseer components and all of the processing in the data collectors. Consequently, almost all information about what is happening with WSAM is stored in sequential log files. Learning the ins and outs of WSAM is mostly a matter of learning how to read and interpret these logs.

5.3.1 WSAM logs

The following log files offer useful information for troubleshooting WSAM, with or without the assistance of the IBM Support team. Some logs are not owned by WSAM itself, but are destinations for WSAM's diagnostic messages.

Logs in TSO/SDSF

WebSphere Application Server's JES2 joblogs and the WebSphere error log are both valuable sources of information about problems in the J2EE server's servant region. The MVS Spool Search and Display Facility (SDSF) can be used to view information in these logs.

WebSphere servant region joblog

The WebSphere J2EE server's servant region's joblog has information that a WSAM Data Collector receives from the Managing Server, and information produced by the WSAM data collectors about their activities. The relevant information is spooled to SYS00001 and SYSOUT.

The information spooled to SYS00001 includes configuration data and variable definitions received from the Managing Server. The information spooled to SYSOUT comes from the WSAM Data Collector itself. It is always a good idea to compare the settings displayed in these logs with the information in the Managing Server's properties files.

WebSphere error log

WSAM does not use this log. It is the standard WebSphere error log. However, it is extremely useful when some feature or component of WebSphere Application Server does not appear to be working correctly. Refer to instructions in the WebSphere Application Server manuals for more information about the log itself. To view it, WSAM supplies a REXX exec in CYN.SCYNPROC for viewing the log. This is not a supported function and is offered "as-is". To view the WebSphere error log using this routine, issue the TSO command:

```
EX 'CYN.SCYNPROC(CYN1ELOG)' 'WAS.ERROR.LOG'
```

If your systems use a WebSphere error log name other than was.error.log, substitute the log filename used at your site. If you are unsure of the log name or are running multiple WebSphere J2EE servant regions, check the JESMSGLG files for the servant regions. The WAS log file name is identified on the BBOU0025I informational message in the JES2 joblogs.

Logs in USS

Logs are created in USS for each WSAM Data Collector.

Where are the logs?

Files for each WebSphere J2EE servant region are located within the WSAM Data Collector <installation directory>, based on the J2EE server's name:

<install path>/wsam/<server>

For example, the location of files for a WebSphere J2EE server named ourserver, when installed in the default WSAM location, is:

/usr/lpp/cyanea/wsam/ourserver

What logs are available?

There are several files associated with each monitored J2EE server:

- etc/<SYSPLEX>.<SYSID>.<server>.datacollector.properties
- etc/<SYSPLEX>.<SYSID>.<server>.bcm.properties
- etc/<SYSPLEX>.<SYSID>.<server>.id
- etc/<SYSPLEX>.SYSID.server.gpsCounter.txt
- etc/cyanea.mod
- logs/datacollector_<date>.log
- logs/cyanea_datacollector.log

The term <SYSPLEX> represents the sysplex name, and <SYSID> represents the z/OS SYSID. (<SYSPLEX>.<SYSID> represents the administrative server's name.).

The first five files are created when the WebSphere J2EE server is started with the Data Collector for the first time, or when the region is restarted after changing WSAM's configuration files (the first five files listed above). If you want to restart the WSAM Data Collector after changing its configuration, you must first delete the five system-generated WSAM configuration files in the /etc directory.

etc/<SYSPLEX>.<SYSID>.<server>.datacollector.properties

This log file contains the same information as the etc/datacollector.properties file, but in an escaped format, and with an additional line for the date. The etc/datacollector.properties file is one of the configuration files for the CICS Data Collector.

etc/<SYSPLEX>.<SYSID>.<server>.bcm.properties

This log file identifies which intercept routines are active. The intercept routines allow WSAM to monitor specific kinds of events, or not. For example, request correlation monitoring will not occur unless certain parameters in this file are set to "yes".

etc/<SYSPLEX>.<SYSID>.<server>.id

This file contains information about how the WSAM Data Collector and its RMI interfaces are known to the Managing Server and its overseer components.

etc/cyanea.mod

This file has the current monitoring level of the CICS Data Collector.

logs/datacollector_<date>.log

WSAM creates and writes messages to this log. It is the principal source of information about the Data Collector apart from the WebSphere JES2 joblog. The log file sequentially records events and anomalies about WSAM's activities as they occur. Some of these events pertain to the connections between the Managing Server and the Data Collector.

The Data Collector log is located in the directory /<installation directory>/wsam/<server>/logs/filename where the filename is constructed as:

- sysplex.machine_name.lpar_name.server_instance_name.yyyymmddhhmmss.address-space-idnumber.datacollector.log

where yyyy=year, mm=month, dd=day, hh=hour, mm=minutes, ss=seconds, address-space-id-number is a decimal.

logs/cyanea_datacollector.log

The cyanea_datacollector.log file will display any errors that occur prior to loading the shared library. If there are no problems before loading the shared library, this log file will not be created.

> **Note:** If the cyanea_datacollector.log file cannot be created in the <installation directory>/logs directory, WSAM attempts to create this log in the directory named /tmp.

CYN1 MVS subsystem log

WSAM creates and writes to this log. The CYN1 MVS subsystem, also called the Common Services Subsystem, uses this log (pointed to by the CYN1 proc for the CYN1 subsystem) to print information regarding the SMF records received and processed by the subsystem. It will display both informational and diagnostic messages as well. For more details on the messages, check the *WSAM Messages and Codes manual.*

See the *WSAM V3.1 Operations Guide* for more information about commands that control the activities of the CYN1 subsystem.

5.3.2 CSAM logs

The following log files provide useful information for troubleshooting CSAM, with or without the assistance of the IBM Support team. Some logs are not owned by CSAM itself, but are destinations for CSAM's diagnostic messages.

Logs in TSO/SDSF

The Spool Search and Display Facility (SDSF) displays information that CSAM receives from the Managing Server, and information produced by the CSAM Data Collector. Relevant information is spooled to SYS00001 and SYSOUT.

The information spooled to SYS00001 includes variable definitions received from the Managing Server. The information spooled to SYSOUT comes from the CSAM Data Collector itself. It is always a good idea to compare the settings displayed in these logs with the information in the Managing Server's properties files.

CICS region joblogs

1. Login to the z/OS Mainframe.
2. Enter the command line arguments to reach SDSF and go to the Display Active panel.
3. Specify the prefix related to your CICS jobs.
4. Select the CICS region with a "?".
5. Select the SYS00001 or SYSOUT spools.
6. Verify the JVM has started by looking at the SYS0001 log.
7. Verify that the CICS region connected to the Managing Server's kernel and publish server in the SYSOUT log.

Note: If there are any problems loading the shared library libcyanea_cics_zos.so, no meaningful messages are displayed in SYS00001, and no SYSOUT messages are created. Verify this by looking at the CSAM datacollector.log file in the USS file system.

Logs in USS

Logs are created in USS for each WSAM Data Collector.

Where are the logs?

Files for each J2EE server are located within the CSAM Data Collector <installation directory>, based on the CICS region's VTAM APPLID:

<install path>/cics/<APPLID>

For example, the location of files for a CICS region with an APPLID of CICS1, if installed in the default location, is:

/usr/lpp/cyanea/cics/cics1

What logs are available?

There are several files associated with each monitored CICS region:

- etc/<SYSPLEX>.<SYSID>.<APPLID>.datacollector.properties
- etc/<SYSPLEX>.<SYSID>.<APPLID>.id
- etc/<SYSPLEX>.SYSID.APPLID.gpsCounter.txt
- etc/cyanea.mod
- logs/datacollector_<date>.log
- logs/cyanea_datacollector.log

The term <SYSPLEX> represents the sysplex name, and <SYSID> represents the z/OS SYSID. (<SYSPLEX>.<SYSID> represents the administrative server's name.).

The first four files are created when CICS/TS region is started with the Data Collector for the first time, or when the region is restarted after changing CSAM's configuration files (the first four files listed above). If you want to restart the IMS Data Collector after changing its configuration, you must first delete the four system-generated CSAM configuration files in the /etc directory.

etc/<SYSPLEX>.<SYSID>.<APPLID>.datacollector.properties

This log file contains the same information as the etc/datacollector.properties file, but in an escaped format, and with an additional line for the date. The etc/datacollector.properties file is one of the configuration files for the CICS Data Collector.

etc/<SYSPLEX>.<SYSID>.<APPLID>.id

This file contains information about how the CICS Data Collector and its RMI interfaces are known to the Managing Server and its overseer components.

etc/cyanea.mod

This file has the current monitoring level of the CICS Data Collector.

logs/datacollector_<date>.log

The <date> is in yyyymmddhhmmss format. This file sequentially records events and anomalies about the Data Collector's activities as they occur.

logs/cyanea_datacollector.log

The cyanea_datacollector.log file will display any errors that occur prior to loading the shared library. If there are no problems before loading the shared library, this log file will not be created.

> **Note:** If the cyanea_datacollector.log file cannot be created in the <installation directory>/logs directory, CSAM attempts to create this log in the directory named /tmp.

CICS auxiliary trace

Another way to obtain troubleshooting information about the CICS Data Collector is to gather up and print a CICS auxiliary trace.

To obtain CICS Data Collector trace information for an active CICS region

1. Login to the CICS region using normal login processes.
2. Check the status of auxiliary tracing by issuing the following command:

   ```
   CEMT INQ AUXTRACE
   ```

3. If the trace is stopped (STO), turn on the trace by overtyping the STO option with STA.
4. Determine whether the auxiliary trace data is written to the DFHAUXT or the DFHBUXT trace dataset.
5. Modify the CYN$PR22 job (for CICS v2.2) or the CYN$PR23 (for CICS v2.3) or the CYN$PR13 job (for CICS v1.3) in the CYN.CICS.SCYNSAM2 dataset to point to the active auxiliary trace dataset for your CICS Region, and set the value of TYPETR. In all cases, the TYPETR value should be:

   ```
   TYPETR=(AP00A8)
   ```

6. Submit the job.

7. Send the output to IBM support.
8. The portions of the CYN$PRT22, CYN$PRT23, or CYN$PRT13 job to be modified are:

```
//STEPLIB DD DSN=<SDFHLOAD dataset>,DISP=SHR
// DD DSN=<SDFHLINK dataset>,DISP=SHR
//AUXTRACE DD DSN=<DFH dataset>,DISP=SHR
```

9. Replace the <SDFHLOAD dataset> and the <SDFHLINK dataset> with the fully qualified names of the CICS datasets for your CICS versions. Verify the names of the CICS datasets with your CICS System programmer:
   - `CICSTS13.CICS.SDFHLOAD and CICSTS13.CICS.SDFHLINK`
   - `CICSTS22.CICS.SDFHLOAD and CICSTS22.CICS.SDFHLINK`
   - `CICSTS23.CICS.SDFHLOAD and CICSTS23.CICS.SDFHLINK`
10. Replace <DFH dataset> with the name of the auxiliary trace data set that pertains to your CICS region:

```
CICSTS22.CICSREGION.DFHAUXT or CICSTS22.CICSREGION.DFHBUXT.
```

To stop auxiliary tracing for an active CICS region:

1. Login to the CICS region using normal login processes.
2. Check the status of auxiliary tracing by issuing the following command:

```
CEMT INQ AUXTRACE
```

3. If the trace is started (STA), then turn off the trace by overtyping the STA option with STO.

5.3.3 ISAM logs

The following log files provide useful information for troubleshooting ISAM, with or without the assistance of the IBM Support team. Some logs are not owned by ISAM itself, but are destinations for ISAM's diagnostic messages.

Logs in TSO/IPSF

The Spool Search and Display Facility (SDSF) displays information that the IMS Data Collector receives from the Managing Server, and information produced by the IMS Data Collector. This Information is spooled to the IMS control region's JES2 SYS00001 and SYSOUT logs.

The information spooled to SYS00001 includes variable definitions received from the Managing Server. The information spooled to SYSOUT comes from the IMS Data Collector; you may want to compare it to the information in the Managing Server's properties files.

To view IMS control region joblogs

1. Login to the z/OS system.
2. Go to the Display Active Panel in SDSF.
3. Select the IMS region with "?"
4. Select the SYS00001 or SYSOUT log.
5. Verify the JVM has started by looking at the SYS00001 log, and verify that the IMS region connected to the kernel, and to the publish server in the SYSOUT log.

Note: If there are any problems loading the shared library (libcyanea_imsxx_zos.so), no meaningful messages will be displayed in SYS00001, and no SYSOUT will be created. You can verify this by looking at the cyanea_datacollector.log file in the USS file system.

You can also view the JESMSGLG log for the selected IMS region and observe the CYN-prefixed log messages reported there.

Logs in USS

Logs are created in USS for each IMS Data Collector.

Where are the logs?

Files for each IMS region are located within the IMS Data Collector installation path, based on the IMS region's IMS ID:

- <install path>/ims/<IMS ID>

For example, the location of files for a IMS region with an IMS ID of IMS1, installed in the default location, is as follows:

- /usr/lpp/cyanea/ims/IMS1

What logs are available?

There are several files associated with each monitored IMS region. In these file names, <IMS Network> represents the value of the cyanea.ims.network property configured in the datacollector.env file, <SYSPLEX> represents the sysplex name, <SYSID> represents the MVS System ID, and <IMS ID> represents the IMS region ID:

- etc/<IMS Network><SYSPLEX>.<SYSID>.<IMS ID>. datacollector.properties
- etc/<IMS Network>.<SYSPLEX>.<SYSID>.<IMS ID>.id
- etc/<IMS Network>.<SYSPLEX>.<SYSID>.<IMS ID>.gpsCounter.txt
- etc/cyanea.mod
- logs/<IMS ID>.<Date>.<Process ID>.datacollector.log
- logs/cyanea_datacollector.log

The first four files are created when the IMS control region is started with the Data Collector for the first time, or when the control region is restarted after changing ISAM's configuration files (the first four files listed above). If you want to restart the IMS Data Collector after changing its configuration, you must first delete the four system-generated ISAM configuration files in the /etc directory.

etc/<IMS Network>.<SYSPLEX>.<SYSID>. <IMS ID>.datacollector.properties

This log file contains the same information as the etc/datacollector.properties file, but in an escaped format, and with an additional line for the date. The etc/datacollector.properties file is one of the configuration files for the IMS Data Collector.

etc/<IMS Network>.<SYSPLEX>.<SYSID>.<IMS ID>.id

This file contains information about how the IMS Data Collector and its RMI interfaces are known to the Managing Server and its components.

logs/<IMS ID>.<Date>.<ASID>.datacollector.log

The <Date> is in MMDDHHMM format, and the <ASID> is the address space ID of the monitored IMS region. The <date> is in yyyymmddhhmmss format. This file sequentially records events and anomalies about the Data Collector's activities as they occur.

logs/cyanea_datacollector.log

The cyanea_datacollector.log file will display any errors that occur prior to loading the shared library. If there are no problems before loading the shared library, this log file will not be created.

Note: If the cyanea_datacollector.log file cannot be created in the <installation directory>/logs directory, ISAM attempts to create this log in the directory named /tmp.

5.3.4 Debug mode

It is possible to run any WSAM Data Collector in debug mode. When a Data Collector is run in debug mode, additional information is produced about what a Data Collector is doing. For WSAM data collectors, these messages are sent to the server or legacy system's SYSOUT spool. Debug mode should be used only when necessary or your SYSOUT spool could fill up.

There are two ways to put a WSAM Data Collector in debug mode:

- Setting cyanea.debug - one way to put a WSAM Data Collector in debug mode is to set cyanea.debug=yes in the datacollector.env file. In order for this to take effect, you must remove several log files and restart the server or legacy system.
- Using dcctl.sh - you can dynamically put the WSAM Data Collector in and out of debug mode by using a program on the Managing Server called dcctl.sh.

5.4 Gathering up WSAM logs and other data

If a problem occurs with WSAM and defies attempts to solve it unassisted, IBM WSAM Support personnel will almost certainly ask for the logs, usually the Managing Server logs, and the Data Collector logs.

Here are some guidelines on the easiest ways to gather these logs:

1. If the error can be recreated easily on test systems, then proceed to empty the /logs directories on the Managing Server and on the affected data collectors; otherwise, go to step 9.
2. Bring the Cyanea overseer components down on the Managing Server.
3. Delete the *.log files in the /opt/cyaneaone/logs directory.
4. Restart the Cyanea overseer components for the MS.
5. Bring down the monitored servers.
6. Delete the *.log files in their /logs directories.
7. Restart the monitored servers.
8. Recreate the problem.
9. Go to the Managing Server and tar up the contents of /opt/cyaneaone/*.
10. FTP the MS tar file in binary mode to your workstation.
11. Go to the distributed Data Collector's host and tar up the contents of opt/cyaneaone/*.

12. Tar up the stdout.log and stderr.log files for the J2EE application server.
13. FTP the distributed Data Collector's tar file in binary mode to your workstation.
14. Go to the z/OS Data Collector's host and tar up the contents of all directories beneath /usr/lpp/cyanea/<wsam/cics/ims>/<server/APPLID/IMS ID>/*.
15. FTP the tar file in binary mode to your workstation.
16. Save the JES joblog for the server into a physical sequential file with an LRECL of 133 bytes.
17. FTP that sequential file in ascii mode to your workstation.
18. Open the sequential file in Wordpad and make sure that it is readable.

By the time you have finished these steps, you have:

- a tar file with the Managing Server's logs, configuration files, and executable files.
- a tar file with the distributed Data Collector's logs, configuration files, and executable files.
- a tar file with the distributed J2EE server's output logs.
- a tar file with the z/OS Data Collector's logs, configuration files, and executable files.
- a tar file with the z/OS server's JES joblog.

ZIP all these files together and place the zipped file on an IBM Support upload site. One such site is download.cyanea.com. This is a "blind FTP site"; contact IBM WSAM Support personnel for the site's userid and password.

5.5 Tools and utilities

These tools and utilities are often used by WSAM Support and Services personnel when installing and working with WSAM. There is no endorsement, explicit or implied, for any of these tools or utilities. They are listed here only to indicate the kinds of tools you need to work most effectively with WSAM:

- The graphical installers for WSAM require Xwindows sessioning capabilities on the targeted host and a workstation with an Xwindows client. Hummingbird's Exceed is one such product.
- An FTP client makes the transferring of files and debugging files easier. WS-FTP is one such tool.
- Telnet clients are used to navigate through file structures on the Managing Server and can be used with OMVS too, of course. SecureCRT is one such product.
- A 3270 emulation tool is needed for mainframe systems, for example, IBM Personal Communications.
- WINZIP is used to package and unpackage zip and tar files.
- Many files in OMVS are ascii-based rather than ebcdic-based. To read and manipulate these files, you must transport them to a workstation, read, and edit them there, and then transport them back to OMVS. Or you can install VIASCII on your MVS/USS system. This implements an ascii editor in OMVS.

5.6 Assorted tips and techniques

These are some general recommendations and tips for WSAM. They are not ranked in any order of importance or significance.

Virtual frame buffer replacement

With the implementation of JDK 1.4.x, there is a new property that removes the need for starting a new Xserver with Virtual Frame Buffer support to provide the graphical environment we need on WSAM's Managing Server for WSAM. The variable is:

- java.awt.headless=true

In the WebSphere administration console, go to:

Application Servers → Cyanea → Process Definition → Java Virtual Machine

and create/update this property with the value of "true". Then recycle the server.

WSAM functions by level

This is a shorthand description of the differences between WSAM monitoring levels:

- Level 1 - Request level data.
- Level 2 - Component level data. This includes the above items, plus SQL, EJB, JNDI, JMS, JCA, Javamail, and MQI.
- Level 3 - Method level data. This includes Level 1 and Level 2, and drills down further to method-level data.

WebSphere DM C9C21149 error (related to first use of PMI)

The problem is communications failure between the J2EE control and servant regions in a WebSphere 50x.xxx ND environment. In this case, the ORB_LISTNER_ADDRESS and ORB_SSL_LISTNER_ADDRESS were set in the control region, but the corresponding PROTOCOL_IIOP_PORT and PROTOCOL_IIOP_PORT_SSL values were not set (default=0).

Solution: In the WebSphere Admin Console, go to:

Application Server → server-in-question → End Points

and check the values specified for the ORB_LISTNERs and write these down. Then navigate to:

Environment → Manage WebSphere Variables

select the appropriate server; select "Apply"; select "New"; proceed to add the two value pairs protocol_iiop_port and protocol_iiop_port_ssl, specifying the port you noted from above.

Reduce the PMI call frequency

The default PMI polling frequency is set to 180 seconds. If you wish to reduce some of the PMI overhead, you can by extending the polling frequency, to approximately every 5 minutes. Log onto the WSAM Administrative Console. Go to:

Administration → Managing Server → System Properties

Change the parameter "System resources Polling Frequency". The value specified is in seconds, so in this example to make the frequency every five minutes, set the value to "300" which is displayed in seconds.

DB2 commands - check database for data

Sometimes when data is not presenting either in PAR or other segments of the WSAM Managing Server, it is helpful to query the database directly to find out if any data is there. Here are a few of the DB2 commands that directly access the database:

- db2 connect to octigate
- db2 list tables
- db2 “select * from request”
- db2 “select * from USERS”; this will display the user ids defined to WSAM. Remember they must be defined to the Operating System.
- db2 “select min(request_id), max(request_id) from request” where range is 1 ? n
- db2 “describe table request”
- db2 “select count (request_id) from request where request_id between 1 and 50000”
- db2 “select * from request where start_time <=‘2004-04-01 00:00:00’ “
- db2 “select * from request where start_time between ‘2004-04-01 00:00:00’ and ‘2004-04-1000:00:00’ “
- db2 “select * from request where start_time between ‘2004-04-01 00:00:00’ and ‘2004-04-1000:00:00’ “

CPU % utilization and time-consumed metrics

Questions often arise at z/OS sites anyway about how WSAM computes “Platform % CPU Utilization”, “JVM CPU % Utilization”, and how “CPU Times” are collected for requests and methods running in WebSphere on z/OS.

Here are the techniques used in z/OS WebSphere:

Platform CPU

The platform CPU utilization is the field CCVUTILP, which is the “system CPU Utilization” as viewed by the System Resource Manager (SRM). Thus, this is the CPU utilization for the entire system, not for any individual LPAR. This field is a plain two-byte number between 0 and 100, which measures the system CPU utilization in “percent busy”. This is a very standard (and IBM recommended) way to get a “snapshot” of the system CPU utilization used by RMF™ and CPU performance monitors. This field is subject to spikes and valleys, as is also true with the global CPU utilization that one gets from the SDSF DA panel of ISPF.

CCVUTILP is part of the System Resource Manager CPU Management Table (CCT) at (offset x’66’). The CCT is pointed to by the RMCTCCT field (offset x’04’) in the SRM Control Table (RMCT). The RMCT is pointed to by the CVTOPCTP field from the CVT (Communications Vector Table).

JVM CPU

The JVM CPU utilization is computed from taking the total (cumulated) CPU time consumed in the JVM address space at two points in time (for example, 2 seconds). The difference of the cumulated CPU (expressed in milliseconds) divided by the elapsed time (in the same units), and divided by the number of processors online gives a snapshot of the CPU percent utilization of the JVM.

The total CPU time consumed in the JVM address space is obtained by directly accessing the SMF record type 79, subtype 2 (address space resource data) from storage in real time, and filtering on the ASID for the JVM, using the RMF data interface service module ERBSMFI.

Note: DB2 time is not included in WSAM measurements. That information would have to be captured via a DB2 system monitor, an MVS monitor, or RMF reporting.

CPU times (in milliseconds)

Requests and methods running in zWAS and on all J2EE platforms are captured using a JVMPI primitive function. The JVMPI function, GetCurrentThreadCpuTime(), returns the CPU time in nanoseconds for the current Java thread. It does this no matter which technique you use to map Java threads to OS threads. Despite the nanosecond resolution, the function is not more precise than the underlying operating system.

Thus, we use a JVMPI primitive function to capture and report on request/method-level CPU times. The JVMPI primitive function returns the CPU time charged to the currently executing Java thread. So, whatever executes under that Java thread is reported by WSAM as the CPU time consumed for the request or method.

What runs under different Java threads is, of course, dependent on the JVM version itself, on runtime options for the JVM, and on third-party proprietary software, like optimizers, running in the JVM. For example, while a request is running, the garbage collector may interfere as necessary and use time in a entirely JVM-dependent manner. With JDK 1.2.2, the garbage collection is done in the user thread, while a system thread does the work with HotSpot. Under HotSpot, the incremental garbage collection cannot run when using an active profiler agent. You can influence the behavior of the garbage collector by calling System.gc(), and by setting initial and maximum heap size when starting the JVM.

This is but one example. If you have additional questions regarding what actually runs on the current Java thread in your zWAS environment, contact IBM WebSphere and Java Support.

Userids other than ADMIN and CYANEA

Here are the UNIX Userid needs on Managing Server for WSAM and Cyanea One Install.

The *WSAM V3.1 Installation Manual* says that the Managing Server requires the creation of two users “cyanea” and “admin”. This tip describes alternate approaches for the userid requirements laid out in the Install Manual:

User “cyanea” is dedicated to the user that starts and stops WSAM’s back-end components. The Install Manual specifies that the profile for the cyanea user is set up to enable such activities. User ”admin” is the default Unix user name that the WSAM visualization engine (VE) uses for login. Both these IDs are configurable; both are not necessarily required.

Scenario 1: Create and Use only One user

Create unix user “cyanea”. Set the profile of the cyanea users as specified in the install manual. Do not set up “admin” user. After running the installer, login as the “cyanea” user into the Managing Server’s operator console and run this command:

```
db2 “update users set username = ‘cyanea', ext_user = ‘cyanea’ where username= 'admin'”
```

Scenario 2: Create and use Unix user other than “admin”

If, for example, you want to use unix user “wsamadm” instead of “admin”, then run the command below as user “cyanea” after a successful run of the graphical or silent installer. Make sure to set up the profile for the “wsamadm” user just as is specified in the WSAM Install Guide for the “admin” user:

```
db2 “update users set username = ‘wsamadm', ext_user = ‘wsamadm’ where username = 'admin'”
```

If you do not want to use “cyanea” as the unix user name for the WSAM administrator, you may use other names as allowed by security at your site. Make sure to follow instructions in the WSAM Install Guide accordingly.

If you do not wish to use ”cyanea” as the owner of the octigate database, then you must update the install scripts as well as grant privileges for the new userid and modify the setenv.sh file with the appropriate userid and password.

SQL not appearing: Data Collector log shows events dropped

On a Linux Data Collector, we were not seeing SQL or JDBC information. In the Data Collector log, we saw the following messages:

Wed Aug 18 12:05:54 2004 INFO: [EventAgent (EventAgent.cc@83)] EventAgentID 0: Events dropped 3454 as they exceeded event queue limit of 5000

To correct this, modify the datacollector.properties files by raising the variable to "internal.probe.event.queue.limit=10000" from 5000 and recycle the server.

AIX memory monitoring

To monitor memory on an AIX system:

svmon -P <pid> -i 60 | grep "work shmat"

where <pid> = the process id of the WAS process.

Output every 60 seconds would look something like this;

```
13392 3 work shmat/mmap - 24407 0 0 24883
a2eb 4 work shmat/mmap - 10435 0 0 10435
142f5 5 work shmat/mmap - 0 0 0 0
162d7 6 work shmat/mmap - 0 0 0 0
```

This shows the storage utilization of each of the 4 256MB segments that make up the "system heap" (that's segments 3,4,5, and 6). The last column indicates the number of 4K pages of virtual storage in use. Closely watching the numbers in the last column... if you see that they all four start to approach 65536, this indicates the impending "out of memory" condition in the system heap.

Database conflicts while trimming

The cause of lockouts during datatrimming is due to database lock escalation, from row to table. Try two things to improve the situation:

- Tune the datatrimmer script to perform frequent COMMITs to release locks. The current script does commits after all qualified records are deleted from a table.
- Tune a database level configuration parameter, LOCKLIST, to improve the situation. You can issue:

  db2 get db cfg for octigate > db.cfg to check current LOCKLIST value.

  db2 update db cfg for octigate using LOCKLIST <a new value> to update LOCKLIST.

If MAXLOCKS = 10, LOCKLIST = 100, then database lock escalation will not happen if an application requires 1000 locks. The LOCKLIST is set to 400 as a default. db2diag.log can tell you if and when database lock escalation happens.

Managing server’s landing page never appears

The Managing Server comes up and all components look good. However, in the WSAM console, the landing page never appears when signing in - the browser just hangs. The solution is to regenerate the HTTP Web server plug-in used by the Managing Server's visualization engine.

Correct environment for running the MS installers

Before running graphical or silent installers on the Managing Server:

1. Verify that you logged in as root
2. Run these commands:

```
export WAS_HOME=/opt/WebSphere/AppServer
export JAVA_HOME=${WAS_HOME}/java
export PATH=${JAVA_HOME}/bin:${PATH}
```

If WebSphere VE is installed on a different box, then change WAS_HOME to that location:

3. Run these commands:

```
echo $WAS_HOME
echo $JAVA_HOME
echo $PATH
```

4. Expect your output to be:

   /opt/WebSphere/AppServer

   /opt/WebSphere/AppServer/java

First entry in the path should read /opt/WebSphere/AppServer/bin.

If any of the above is not as specified, then the install program will fail.

Managing Server tips to sustain large traces

To sustain large amount of trace, we need to increase the managing device.

- Increase the method count limit of publish server:

Publish server will truncate method trace larger than a specified number. To increase the limit, change methodCount=10000 to methodCount=50000 in /opt/cyaneaone/etc/ps1.properties and /opt/cyaneaone/etc/ps2.properties files.

- Increase the Java heap size of archive agent:

The runtime memory of archive agent needed to be increased as potentially bigger method trace from publish server. Set HEAP_MIN_SIZE_ARCHIVE_AGENT=1024 and HEAP_MAX_SIZE_ARCHIVE_AGENT=2048 in file /opt/cyaneaone/bin/setenv.sh to increase the Java heap size.

- Reduce the batch size of archive agent:

The archive agent will try to batch process a specified number of requests, the default is 10 requests. It will hit the limit of DB2 driver with the large requests. Change REQUESTDATA_BUFFER_THRESHOLD=10 to REQUESTDATA_BUFFER_THRESHOLD=1 in /opt/cyaneaone/etc/aa.properties.

- Increase the Java & JNI stack size of archive agent:

Even one big request may still hit the DB2 driver limit. To avoid it, add -Xoss8M and -Xss8M in the Java startup command. i.e. ${JAVA_HOME}/bin/java -classpath $CLASSPATH -Xoss8M -Xss8M \ in /opt/cyaneaone/bin/aactl.

- Increase the query heap size of DB2:

Also increase the query heap size of the DB2 server to accommodate the large batch query from archive agent. To do so, issue db2 update dbm cfg using query_heap_sz 8000 using user db2inst1.

How to connect to publish servers

If the Data Collector is repeatedly trying to contact the publish server as evident from the logs, then this solution may apply:

This problem may be because the Data Collector is unable to resolve the MS host name passed to it at startup time by the Managing Server's kernels. Check the file setenv.sh in the /bin directory for the variables:

KERNEL_HOST01=www.mshost.com

KERNEL_HOST02=www.mshost.com

If, as in the above example, they refer to the Managing Server's DNS name, change them to specify the IP address. Save the setenv.sh file. (You can use the # sign to comment out lines if you would much rather make a copy of the lines and then change them.)

As "cyanea" user run in the /bin

>cyanea-stop.sh

and then

>cyanea-start.sh

Your problem should be solved and the Data Collector and the Managing Server should be communicating.

Remote debugger

The remote debugger or other monitors cannot run concurrently with WSAM.

Package and class filtering

Is there a way to include specific packages like com.ibm.connector2.* in a level 3 trace, so we can get method entry and exit timings for them?

In the datacollector.env file, there is a set of variables that controls which classes are method traced. The classes_not_to_trace variable is an exclusion list of classes that will not be method traced. You can modify this variable to include the desired IBM methods. classes_to_trace provides an "opt-in" for classes that are not part of your application path, which is what is included in application method traces by default.

Codebase or classpath error

If in the process of installing WSAM 3.1 on z/OS, when using WebSphere z/OS 5.1.0, and after implementing WSAM in an application server, we recycle the server and get the following messages when it tries to connect to the Managing Server:

Unable to join Kernel eisclt01.csm.fub.com:9121 - Error occurred in server java.lang.NoClassDefFoundError: com/cyanea/probe/ControllerAVM

Response

The correct value for the java.rmi.server.codebase property is very important. Here is the value that is listed there:

In **Process Definition** → **Servant** → **JVM** → **Custom Properties**, use the following property value for zWAS510 support:

- Name: java.rmi.server.codebase
- Value: 'file:///opt/cyaneaone/<libversion>/ppe.zprobe.jar file:///opt/cyaneaone/lib/ppe.probe-intf.jar file:///opt/cyaneaone/<libversion>/ppe.zws510.jar'

Note those changes should be made in the admin console. Also, note:

- <libversion> is the Application Monitor version information. For example, for this installation, use lib3.1 which refers to libraries of WSAM V3.1.
- Two single quotes are used to wrap the entire string.
- There is a space between every two file URLs. Since there are three file URLs in the string, there are two spaces inside the single-quoted string.
- If this string has incorrect syntax, the J2EE server's JVM is not attached by WebSphere correctly and results in a CEE DUMP.

6

Firewalls and ports

If there is a firewall between the WSAM Managing Server and a WSAM Data Collector, then special rules about TCP network ports apply. The Managing Server owns and opens ten ports for communications with data collectors. Each Data Collector owns and opens two RMI ports.

Graphically, this framework looks like Figure 6-1 on page 88, where a Managing Server on the left watches the processing of sheltered data collectors on the right: Two distributed servers and two more servers on a mainframe, all located behind a firewall. The port numbers are located adjacent to the servers or platforms that own and open them. A communications line from a server to a set of port numbers identifies the server and the direction across the firewall from which sessions are started on those ports.

Figure 6-1 on page 88 is completely generic: It does not matter what kinds of WSAM components are involved - distributed or mainframe; WebSphere, CICS, or IMS - the same rules apply. If a firewall exists between a Managing Server and a Data Collector, then the ports identified below, or their substitutions, must be configured to accommodate WSAM traffic flowing through them in both directions.

Figure 6-1 on page 88 is also based on a single-platform Managing Server where all the MS parts are on the same box. If the Managing Server resides on multiple platforms and any of the MS boxes reside on opposite sides of the firewall, then more rules about other ports apply too. Contact the IBM WSAM Support and Services team for more information about these environments.

© Copyright IBM Corp. 2005. All rights reserved.

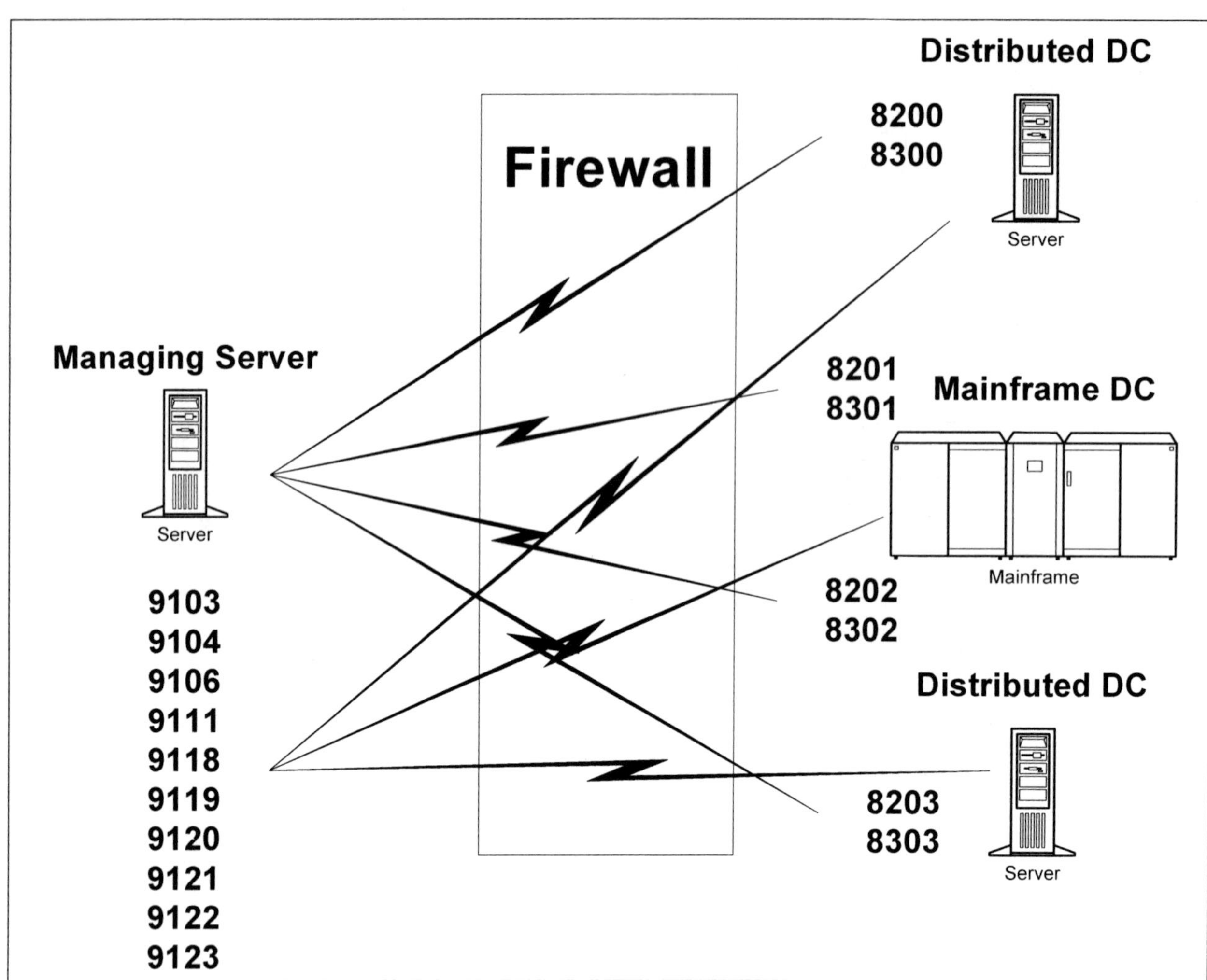

Figure 6-1 Servers, firewalls, and ports

Firewalls and the rules governing them can vary across different sites. Table 6-1 identifies what default ports are needed on the Managing Server, and the ranges of default ports needed for the data collectors. Some firewalls base their rules on who "opens" a port; others derive their rules from who initiates or starts a session with an opened port.

Both situations are explained in Figure 6-1 on page 89. Bear in mind that, for all these ports, once they are opened and sessions are started on them, it must be possible for WSAM traffic to flow through each port in both directions.

Table 6-1 Port information

Port	Port owned and opened by	Session with port started by
9103	Publish Server port on MS	Data Collector
9104	Publish Server port on MS	Data Collector
9106	Message Dispatcher port on MS	SMTP/SNMP Host
9111	Polling Agent port on MS	HTTP Web Server
9118	Kernel RMI port on MS	Data Collector
9119	Kernel RMI port on MS	Data Collector
9120	Kernel RMI port on MS	Data Collector
9121	Kernel RMI port on MS	Data Collector
9122	Kernel HTTP Codebase port on MS	Data Collector
9123	Kernel HTTP Codebase port on MS	Data Collector
8200-8299	Probe RMI port on DC	Managing Server
8300-8399	Probe Controller RMI port on DC	Managing Server
8700-8799	Probe RMI port on DC (for CICS and IMS)	Managing Server
8800-8899	Probe Controller RMI port on DC (for CICS and IMS)	Managing Server

6.1 Firewalls and Native Address Translation

Native Address Translation is known as NAT. If NAT is turned on in the firewall, then pseudo-IP addresses are translated into actual IP addresses as traffic flows through the firewall. For example, if the Managing Server is cloistered behind a pseudo-IP address, then it cannot be reached using its actual IP address. This can cause problems for WSAM's components when they attempt to communicate with one another.

In this case, switch to using the hostname of the Managing Server instead of its IP address. On the Managing Server, follow these steps:

1. First, update the setenv.sh file in the /bin directory:

   cd <cyanea home>/bin

   vi setenv.sh

   Under the line with the variable KERNEL_HOST02, add another variable:

   MS_HOST=<fully qualified hostname of the Managing Server>

   save your changes to setenv.sh

2. The next steps are to edit the psctl.sh, wdctl.sh and klctl.sh scripts in the /bin directory too:

   a. psctl.sh

      i. Look for the following lines in psctl.sh

      ```
      -Dnodeauth.ip=$NODE_IP \
      com.cyanea.publish.PsCtl start  &
      ```

      ii. change this by adding a new system property to the PS:

      ```
      -Dnodeauth.ip=$NODE_IP \
      -Djava.rmi.server.hostname=<fully qualified host name of MS, for example
      ms.cust.com> \
      com.cyanea.publish.PsCtl start  &
      ```

   b. wdctl.sh

      i. Look for the following lines in wdctl.sh

      ```
      -Dnodeauth.ip=$NODE_IP \
      com.cyanea.kernel.util.KernelManager start ${KERNEL_NAME} &
      ```

      ii. change this by adding a new line

      ```
      -Dnodeauth.ip=$NODE_IP \
      -Djava.rmi.server.hostname=<fully qualified host name of MS, for example
      ms.rbos.com> \
      com.cyanea.kernel.util.KernelManager start ${KERNEL_NAME} &
      ```

   c. klctl.sh

      i. Look for the following lines in klctl.sh

      ```
      -Dproperties.filename=${KERNEL_PROPERTIES} \
      com.cyanea.kernel.util.KernelManager start ${KERNEL_NAME} &
      ```

      ii. change this by adding a new line:

      ```
      -Dproperties.filename=${KERNEL_PROPERTIES} \
      -Djava.rmi.server.hostname=<fully qualified host name of MS, for example
      ms.cust.com> \
      com.cyanea.kernel.util.KernelManager start ${KERNEL_NAME} &
      ```

6.2 Changes on the Data Collector machine

- Make sure that the DC machine can access the Managing Server by using the hostname of MS (the hostname we set in the scripts above, for example, <fully qualified host name of MS, for example, ms.cust.com>).
  - One way of verifying this is by pinging the MS from the DC machine: "ping <fully qualified host name of MS, for example, ms.cust.com>"
- Then change the Data Collector properties files on the DC machine:
  - kernel.codebase=http://<MS ip/hostname>:9122/kernel.core.jar http://<MS I/hostname>::9123/kernel.core.jar
  - kernel.rfs.address=<MS ip/hostname>:9120 <MS ip/hostname>:9121

Make sure that <MS ip/hostname> is the fully qualified hostname of MS (and not the IP address of the MS), for example, <fully qualified host name of MS, for example, ms.cust.com>

As a further precautionary measure, look into all the properties files on the DC machine (in the .../etc directory) and change the IP address of the MS in all the places - wherever it appears - with the MS hostname.

Part 1

Appendixes

© Copyright IBM Corp. 2005. All rights reserved.

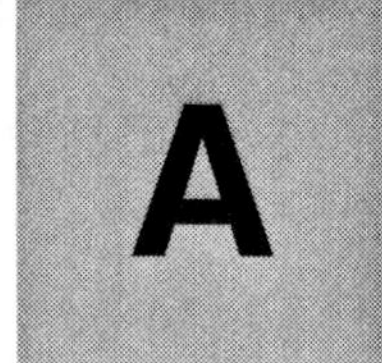

Database setting information

Notes:

1. Identify the correct database name to use and substitute it for octigate in the commands described below.
2. Run "db2 get dbm cfg" as the db2inst1 user to see the existing database manager configuration settings.
3. The following will update the database manager configuration settings to the values used internally by WSAM.
4. Also run the command "db2empfa octigate" to enable multi-page file allocation for the octigate database.

```
update dbm cfg using authentication client;
update dbm cfg using intra_parallel yes;
update dbm cfg using query_heap_sz 2000;

update db cfg for octigate using dbheap 9600;
update db cfg for octigate using logfilsiz 25000;
update db cfg for octigate using maxappls 100;
update db cfg for octigate using applheapsz 1000;
update db cfg for octigate using locktimeout 60;
update db cfg for octigate using dft_degree any;

update dbm cfg using SHEAPTHRES 40000;
```

© Copyright IBM Corp. 2005. All rights reserved.

```
update dbm cfg using FCM_NUM_RQB 768;
update dbm cfg using MAXAGENTS 300;
update db cfg for octigate using BUFFPAGE 30000;
update db cfg for octigate using CATALOGCACHE_SZ 5120;
update db cfg for octigate using LOGBUFSZ 256;
update db cfg for octigate using LOCKLIST 1000;
update db cfg for octigate using MAXLOCKS 50;
update db cfg for octigate using AVG_APPLS 20;
update db cfg for octigate using SORTHEAP 20000;
update db cfg for octigate using LOGPRIMARY 5;
update db cfg for octigate using LOGSECOND 4;
update db cfg for octigate using NUM_IOCLEANERS 3;
```

Security: Node authentication

Overview

This Attachment illustrates the design and implementation of node authentication and secure transmission among WSAM components. This document addresses various security issues encountered during client/server communication over TCP/IP.

Design effort is made to address the following issues:

- Eavesdropping: Privacy of information is compromised, although the information may remain intact. This could happen if the information on the wire is intercepted by a middleman. Eavesdropping is addressed by encrypting data before sending it, and decrypting data after receiving it.
- Tampering: Information may be modified or replaced while in transit, and then relayed to the recipient instead of the original content. One solution is to fingerprint the data, using a one way hash, and to verify the fingerprint on the receiving end.
- Impersonation: Information is sent to a person who acts as the intended recipient. This takes two forms:
  - Spoofing-A person or a computer pretends to be someone else.
  - Misrepresentation-A person or computer misrepresents itself. A computer acts as a true representative of a site and accepts request intended for the actual Web site.

These problems can be handled using certificates and by performing both client-side as well as server-side authentication. Negotiation verifies the authenticity of the communicating ends. This way both ends can be sure that the data is being received by the correct system or person.

Design description

All WSAM components must communicate with each other in a reliable manner. To achieve this, WSAM components perform a handshake and authenticate on both ends before they establish a session, using the X.509 certificate-based authentication model.

© Copyright IBM Corp. 2005. All rights reserved.

A certificate-based model is the most appropriate design choice because it addresses client-server authenticity without transmitting passwords via public key encryption. This enhances security because the password in never transmitted. There are many certificate-based authentication models like Pretty Good Privacy (PGP) certificates, Simple Distributed Security Infrastructure (SDSI) certificates and X.509 certificates. But X.509 was chosen because it is an international standard created by the International Telecommunication Union (ITU) and is supported by Java.

Other design considerations

Security is enabled on an optional basis on both Managing Server components and Data Collectors. That is, there is two-way authentication: From Managing Server components to Data Collectors, and from Data Collectors to Managing Server Components. Enabling security in each direction is independent of the other:

- When security is enabled on Managing Server components, all Data Collectors must be security-enabled to communicate with it. The Managing Server does *not* operate in mixed mode (security-enabled as well as non-security-enabled Data Collectors) for “inbound” communication from Data Collectors. This restriction helps prevent any security back doors from being opened.
- However, each Data Collector can be independently configured as security-enabled or security-disabled with respect to communication from the Managing Server components. In this sense, the "outbound" communication from the Managing Server can be in "mixed mode.”

There are two reasons we use X.509 certificates rather than Secure Sockets Layer (SSL) (even though SSL provides an out-of-the-box solution): Using SSL would require WSAM components to have appropriate licensed libraries, and SSL communication overhead would cause performance degradation.

Data transmitted across WSAM components is not encrypted by default. However, users can enable it on demand. The trade-off is that unencrypted data is not confidential, while encrypted communication may pose performance overhead.

Effort is made to use self-signed certificates issued by WSAM, rather than the Certificate Authority (CA). This way, CA-based intervention is avoided.

Currently, WSAM components do not perform any role-based operations. However, effort has been made to allow for easy integration of this requirement into the product. JAAS may be an appropriate design choice for a role-based authentication model.

Backward compatibility with older Data Collectors has been considered.

Backward compatibility with Proxy server architecture has been considered.

Implementation details

In this section, we discuss three types of certificates used by WSAM.

Certificate usage

There are three X.509 certificates generated and self-signed by WSAM:

- A certificate used by Managing Server components communicating with Data Collectors.
- A certificate used by Managing Server components (other than the Kernel) communicating with the Kernel.

- A certificate used by Data Collectors communicating with the Kernel.

Among the many attributes that come with a X.509 certificate, the following are the important attributes of interest:

WSAM Data Collector Certificate

Issued to: WSAMDC

Public key: WSAMManagement public key

Issued by: WSAM designated Certificate Authority

Validity date:

Issuer Thumbprint:

WSAM Management Certificate

Issued to: WSAMMgmt

Public key: WSAMDC public key

Issued by: WSAM designated Certificate Authority

Validity date:

Issuer Thumbprint:

Management Server component communication

Although all WSAM components communicate in the same manner, the certificates they use differ.

For components communicating with the Kernel, the certificates are signed and decrypted by the Managing server component private keys. The certificates that are exchanged to verify authenticity are the WSAM Management Certificates (rather than the WSAM Data Collector certificate.)

Component level security

All WSAM components (including Managing Server components other than the Kernel, as well as Data Collectors) use the Kernel as an RMI registry. When components start, they register with the Kernel. Only after registering, do they become visible to other components.

During registration, each component does a security handshake with the Kernel using X.509 certificate verification on both ends. This confirms that the component being registered is authentic. Once the authenticity is verified, the Kernel stores the RMI stub of the client component in its registry, to be used by other authenticated clients. All clients communicating with the Kernel must first get authenticated in this way before they can communicate with the Kernel.

Since the Kernel acts as central office through which all components communicate, security authentication at the Kernel level is sufficient to maintain secure communication among all WSAM components. All WSAM components communicate via RMI, so a strict and extensive secure hand shake before obtaining an RMI proxy is sufficient to verify the authenticity of the client. Therefore, one-time authentication is sufficient, as opposed to authenticating every RMI call, which might degrade performance.

Verifying authenticity of the certificate

Verifying authenticity of the certificate is done in two stages to be extensive:

Step 1: X.509 certificate authentication

1. A client sends a public certificate of the server to the server. The server verifies the certificate's sanity with the public key of the certificate. Please Note: all certificates used are self-signed certificates. If the certificate is altered, the footprint of the certificate will differ from the footprint generated via the public key of the certificate.
2. If the above verification passes, then the footprint of the certificate is compared with the footprint stored on the server side. This confirms the authenticity of the certificate.
3. The certificate's expiration dates are checked to verify its validity.
4. The certificate's subject is checked to verify whether or not the client is using the proper certificate.

Step 2: Common data verification via MD5withRSA

1. The client also sends its signature, generated by signing user id with its private key using RSA and the MD5 algorithm.
2. The server verifies the signature using the public key, obtained via the client's public certificate stored on the server. This verifies whether or not the client is authentic.

Node authentication configuration

Any WSAM component, whether the Managing Server components or an individual Data Collector, can operate in secure mode. Secure mode, with respect to a particular component, is with regard to communication from other components to the component in question.

Configuration changes are similar for all components, which are specified in a property called security.enabled, which is defined in the component's properties file.

Kernel-related configuration

The following examples are from a kernel properties file (kl1.properties and kl2.properties). Note that all these properties are already documented in the property files. We recommend that you simply uncomment the data and specify the appropriate values.

```
#To enable Kernel to operate in secure mode
security.enabled=true

# Only when this property is true along with above property, then
# CodeBase server will operate in secure mode
codebase.security.enabled=true

# define CYANEA_HOME accordingly
# Path of the certificate to use when talking to the Data Collector
# This is needed only when the Data Collector is operating secure mode
certificate.path=$CYANEA_HOME/etc/formgmt.cer

# Keystore location of the management server
keystore.location=$CYANEA_HOME/etc/CyaneaMgmtStore
```

The following are other properties that you do not need to change, because they are set by default. However, they may need to be changed when a specific situation arises:

```
# For backward compatibility of old Data Collectors to work with a new security-enabled
Kernel
# ipaddresses need to be separated by ':'
```

```
#cyanea.trustedips=192.168.3.84:127.0.0.1

# Keystore location of the management server
keystore.location=/opt/cyaneaone/etc/CyaneaMgmtStore

# Keystore password of management server
keystore.storepass=cyanea94612

# Keystore key password of management server
keystore.keypass=cyanea94612

# user id passed to other end for authentication
nodeauth.userid=cyaneamgmt

# When there are multiple I/O cards, if you want to use specific
# ip for code base server authentication
#nodeauth.ip=
```

Data Collector-related configuration

The following examples are from a datacollector.properties file. Note that all these properties are already documented in the file. We recommend that you simply uncomment the data and specify the appropriate values.

```
#To enable the Data Collector to operate in secure mode
security.enabled=true

# Define CYANEA_HOME accordingly.
# Path of the certificate to use when talking to the Kernel
# This is needed only when the Data Collector is operating secure mode
certificate.path=$CYANEA_HOME/etc/fordc.cer

# Keystore location of the Data Collector
keystore.location=$CYANEA_HOME/etc/CyaneaDCStore
```

The following are other properties that you do not need to change, because they are set by default. However, they may need to be changed when a specific situation arises:

```
# Keystore password of Data Collector server
keystore.storepass=oakland94612

# Keystore key password of Data Collector server
keystore.keypass=oakland94612

# user id passed to other end for authentication
nodeauth.userid=cyaneadc
```

Keystore management and populating certificates

You do not have to do the following unless you want to integrate using your own keystore.

To populate the Managing Server keystore

Replace cyanea94612 with appropriate passwords and CyaneaMgmtStore with appropriate storefile.

```
keytool -genkey -alias mgmtmgmt -keyalg RSA -keysize 1024 -sigalg MD5withRSA -validity 2000
-keypass cyanea94612 -keystore ./CyaneaMgmtStore  -storepass cyanea94612 -dname
"cn=mgmtmgmt, OU=CyaneaComp, O=Cyanea, L=Oakland, ST=CA, C=US"
```

```
keytool -genkey -alias fordc -keyalg RSA -keysize 1024 -sigalg MD5withRSA -validity 2000
-keypass cyanea94612 -keystore ./CyaneaMgmtStore  -storepass cyanea94612 -dname
"cn=cyaneadc, OU=CyaneaComp, O=Cyanea, L=Oakland, ST=CA, C=US"
```

To populate the Data Collector keystore

Replace oakland94612 with appropriate passwords and CyaneaDCStore with appropriate storefile.

```
keytool -genkey -alias formgmt -keyalg RSA -keysize 1024 -sigalg MD5withRSA -validity 2000
-keypass oakland94612 -keystore ./CyaneaDCStore  -storepass oakland94612 -dname
"cn=cyaneamgmt, OU=CyaneaComp, O=Cyanea, L=Oakland, ST=CA, C=US"
```

To populate mgmtmgmt.cer, fordc.cer, and formgmt.cer

Replace cyanea94612 and oakland94612 with appropriate passwords, and CyaneaMgmtStore and CyaneaDCStore with appropriate storefiles.

```
$CYANEA_HOME/bin/keygen.sh ./CyaneaMgmtStore cyanea94612 mgmtmgmt cyanea94612 mgmtmgmt.cer,
mgmtmgmt.privkey, mgmtmgmt.thumbprint

$CYANEA_HOME/bin/keygen.sh./CyaneaMgmtStore cyanea94612 fordc cyanea94612 fordc.cer,
fordc.privkey, fordc.thumbprint

$CYANEA_HOME/bin/keygen.sh./CyaneaDCStore oakland94612 formgmt oakland94612 formgmt.cer,
formgmt.privkey, formgmt.thumbprint
```

Multi-Box Managing Server installation

In multiple box installation you may have database (DB), visualization engine (VE), managing server components 1 (Kernel1, PS1, AA1) (MS1) and managing server components 2 (Kernel2, PS2 and AA2) (MS2) on separate systems.

Tasks to be performed for multiple box installation of Managing Server:

1. Run the installer on VE machine. Make sure, you enter correct hostnames for various MS components. Also do not create local database.
2. Create the database and populate on DB machine.
3. Replicate the /opt/cyaneaone directory on MS1 and MS2 machines.
4. Catalog the database from MS1, MS2 and VE machines.
5. Modify cyanea-start.sh and cyanea-stop.sh scripts on MS1 and MS2 to start only local components for that system.
6. Verify that hostnames are correct in setenv.sh and in ve.properties. It is also important to use the same CYANEA_HOME directory on various MS boxes. If you choose to use another directory, you have to modify it in properties files.

Example for a multi-box MS installation

The following is an example setup as shown in Figure C-1 on page 104.

© Copyright IBM Corp. 2005. All rights reserved.

Machine	FEATURES INSTALLED
DB2-BOX01	Database server
MS-BOX01	Managing Server01: Kernel 1, Publish Server 1, Achieve Agent 1
MS-BOX02	Managing Server02: Kernel 2, Publish Server 2, Achieve Agent 2, MD (message dispatcher), PA (polling agent),
VE-BOX01	WebSphere/VE Components

Figure C-1 Multi-box installation example

Before you start

Prior to starting the installation define the necessary O/S level users on various machines and make sure the logon profile for each is setup as defined in the WSAM Installation Guide. (Userids "cyanea" and "admin" with passwords of "password" on each of the boxes to the UNIX operating system.)

Log on to VE-BOX01 Server

Perform the normal installation on VE-BOX01 machine. During the installation, uncheck the checkbox for "Create Local Database", and mark the checkbox for "Install Visualization Engine". Also, enter machine name/IP address for MS-BOX01 for Kernel and enter machine name/IP address for MS-BOX02 for Kernel 2. After installation is complete, restart the WebSphere server.

After installation on VE_BOX01, tar up the destination directory /opt/cyaneaone/. FTP the tar file to MS-BOX01, MS-BOX02 and DB-BOX01 machines, and replicate /opt/cyaneaone/ on MS-BOX01 and MS-BOX02 machines.

Log on to DB-BOX01 Server

On DB-BOX01, perform following actions:

- Untar the file you just FTPed.
- As user "root", edit the file /etc/sysctl.conf to add the line: "kernel.msgmni=1024".
- Logon as the DB2 administrative user, e.g. "su - db2inst1"
- Edit the file /etc/services. In the # Local services section verify the following line appears; if not create it and save the file.

```
# Local services

db2cdb2inst1    50000/tcp   # Connection port for DB2 instance db2inst1
```

- Verify if DB2 is running. Issue the command ps -ef | grep db2

If there are no DB2 processes start DB2 with the command db2start

- Verify there is not a database "octigate". Issue the following command db2 list db directory (make sure there is no "octigate")
- Create the database catalog by issuing the following command: db2 create db octigate
- Log onto the userid "cyanea" with the command su - cyanea
- Populate the "octigate" database by running the following commands:
  - db2 connect to octigate
  - db2 -tf /opt/cyaneaone/etc/cyaneaone-db2.sql
  - su - db2inst1

- db2 connect to octigate
- db2 -tf /opt/cyaneaone/etc/dbsettings.sql
- exit

Log onto the MS-BOX02 server

Create the database catalog:

- Log onto the MS-BOX02 system as root
- Switch to the DB2 administrator userid: su - db2inst1
- Issue the command:

```
db2 catalog tcpip node db2node remote DB2-BOX01 server 50000
```

(where DB2-BOX01 is the remote address of the database machine)

- Issue the command: db2 catalog db octigate at node db2node
- To verify the creating of the octigate database issue the command: db2 list db directory
- Issue the command: db2 connect to octigate user cyanea using <password>
- Expect to see the Octigate database alias.

```
Database Connection Information
Database server        = DB2/LINUX 7.2.5
SQL authorization ID   = CYANEA
Local database alias   = OCTIGATE
```

Replicating the cyaneaone directory on MS-BOX02

- As user root
- extract the TAR file (cyaneaone.tar) in the same location as the other machine: /opt/cyaneone
- tar -xvf cyaneaone.tar
- all the files are owned by root, so change the ownership
- chown -R cyanea cyaneaone
- cd bin
- chown root authenticate_lnx(if you are on aix, it would be authenticate_aix, etc).
- chmod u+s authenticate_lnx
- cd /opt/cyaneaone/bin
- vi setenv.sh

Edit and add a value for the JDBC_DRIVER as follows:

```
JDBC_DRIVER_NAME=COM.ibm.db2.jdbc.app.DB2Driver
JDBC_DRIVER_JAR=/home/db2inst1/sqllib/java12/db2java.zip
JDBC_DRIVER_URL=jdbc:db2:octigate
JDBC_USER=cyanea
JDBC_PASSWORD=password
```

On MS-BOX01 Server

- su - db2inst1

Create the database catalog:

- db2 catalog tcpip node db2node remote DB2-BOX01 server 50000

(where DB2-BOX01 is the remote address of the database machine)

- db2 catalog db octigate at node db2node (NOTE: db2node same as name from first command)
- db2 list db directory (to show that this was created - the octigate database.)
- db2 connect to octigate user cyanea using password

Expect to see the Octigate database alias.

Database Connection Information:

```
Database server        = DB2/LINUX 7.2.5
SQL authorization ID   = CYANEA
Local database alias   = OCTIGATE
```

Replicating the cyaneaone directory on MS-BOX01:

- As user root
- extract the TAR file (cyaneaone.tar) in the same location as the other machine: /opt/cyaneone
- tar -xvf cyaneaone.tar
- all the files are owned by root, so change the ownership
- chown -R cyanea cyaneaone
- cd bin
- chown root authenticate_lnx(if you are on aix, it would be authenticate_aix, etc).
- chmod u+s authenticate_lnx
- cd /opt/cyaneaone/bin
- vi setenv.sh

Edit and add a value for the JDBC_DRIVER as seen below:

```
JDBC_DRIVER_NAME=COM.ibm.db2.jdbc.app.DB2Driver
JDBC_DRIVER_JAR=/home/db2inst1/sqllib/java12/db2java.zip
JDBC_DRIVER_URL=jdbc:db2:octigate
JDBC_USER=cyanea
JDBC_PASSWORD=password
```

On VE-BOX01

Create the database catalog:

- su - db2inst1
- db2 catalog tcpip node db2node remote DB2-BOX01 server 50000

(where DB2-BOX01 is the remote address of the database machine)

- db2 catalog db octigate at node db2node (NOTE: db2node same as name from first command)
- db2 list db directory (to show that this was created - the octigate database.)
- db2 connect to octigate user cyanea using password

Expect to see the Octigate database alias.

Database Connection Information:

```
Database server        = DB2/LINUX 7.2.5
```

```
SQL authorization ID    = CYANEA
Local database alias    = OCTIGATE
```

Check the DataSource in WebSphere

- Bring up the WebSphere admin console to validate the connection was created, and to test the database connection)
- cd /opt/WebSphere/ApplicationServer/bin
- ./adminclient.sh
- Resources -> JDBC Providers
- Do you have a CyaneaDriver created here? If not, create one, and under CyaneaDriver,
- Under CyaneaDriver, look for "Data Sources" and highlight it.
- Look for a datasource called CyaneaDataSource. If the datasource was not created, create one with the following information (5 pieces of information)

```
Name:  CyaneaDataSource
JNDI Name:  jdbc/CyaneaDataSource
database name:octigate
user cyanea
password <password>
```

Click on the Test Connection button to test the connection.

Configuring the components of the managing server for MS-BOX01:

- su - cyanea
- cd /opt/cyaneaone/bin
- vi cyanea-start.sh
- At the bottom of the file, see the #Start components.
- Comment out the components we don't want running on this box. Comment out: aa2, ps2, md, pa, sam1, kl2. To comment them out, put a # in front of the line of the component we do not want to run on this box.

```
# Start components.

${CYANEA_HOME}/bin/cyaneactl.sh kl1 start
sleep 1
#${CYANEA_HOME}/bin/cyaneactl.sh kl2 start
sleep 5

#${CYANEA_HOME}/bin/lmgrd -c ${CYANEA_HOME}/etc/license.dat -l
${CYANEA_HOME}/logs/cyaneaone_ls.log

${CYANEA_HOME}/bin/cyaneactl.sh aa1 start
#${CYANEA_HOME}/bin/cyaneactl.sh aa2 start
${CYANEA_HOME}/bin/cyaneactl.sh ps1 start
#${CYANEA_HOME}/bin/cyaneactl.sh ps2 start
#${CYANEA_HOME}/bin/cyaneactl.sh md start
#${CYANEA_HOME}/bin/cyaneactl.sh pa start
#${CYANEA_HOME}/bin/cyaneactl.sh sam1 start
```

- save the file
- try it out.
- su - cyanea
- ./cyanea-start.sh

Configuring the components of the managing server for MS-BOX01:

- su - cyanea
- cd /opt/cyaneaone/bin
- vi cyanea-start.sh
- At the bottom of the file, see the #Start components.
- Comment: kl1, aa1, ps1, put a "#" in front on those features. Just like the other commented out stuff.

MS-BOX02:

```
# Start components.

#${CYANEA_HOME}/bin/cyaneactl.sh kl1 start
sleep 1
${CYANEA_HOME}/bin/cyaneactl.sh kl2 start
sleep 5

#${CYANEA_HOME}/bin/lmgrd -c ${CYANEA_HOME}/etc/license.dat -l
${CYANEA_HOME}/logs/cyaneaone_ls.log

#${CYANEA_HOME}/bin/cyaneactl.sh aa1 start
${CYANEA_HOME}/bin/cyaneactl.sh aa2 start
#${CYANEA_HOME}/bin/cyaneactl.sh ps1 start
${CYANEA_HOME}/bin/cyaneactl.sh ps2 start
${CYANEA_HOME}/bin/cyaneactl.sh md start
${CYANEA_HOME}/bin/cyaneactl.sh pa start
```

${CYANEA_HOME}/bin/cyaneactl.sh sam1 start

> **Note:** Ignore the SocketException that you might get while starting MS. It is caused by Kernel on the other machine still not being up, when various MS components on first machine start. As the second Kernel starts, it will go away.

Test the multi-box Managing Server:

- Bring up WSAM console:
- Login onto the WSAM login screen (user/password)
- Administration -> Managing Server -> Self-Diagnosis

Check through each of the list under application monitor, make sure that each piece is running on the right box.

- Configure a Data Collector to verify the setup.

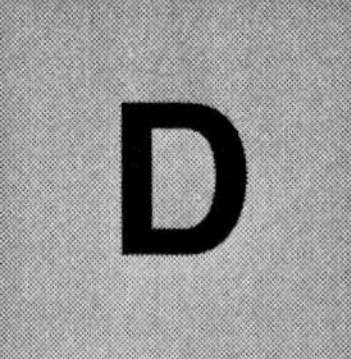

WSAM sample installation project plan

The following high level sample installation project plan is presented as a starting point. The number of days to complete a task are a reasonable estimate based on numerous installation experiences.

© Copyright IBM Corp. 2005. All rights reserved.

Task Name	Duration	Start	Finish
SAMPLE WSAM ROLLOUT TIMELINE	**38 days?**	**Mon 1/3/05**	**Wed 2/23/05**
Project Management	**16 days**	**Mon 1/3/05**	**Mon 1/24/05**
Define WSAM Project Manager	1 day	Mon 1/24/05	Mon 1/24/05
Define z/OS owner	1 day	Mon 1/3/05	Mon 1/3/05
Define Distributed owner	1 day	Mon 1/3/05	Mon 1/3/05
Define Monitoring roles	1 day	Mon 1/3/05	Mon 1/3/05
Build Application Implementation Schedule	**22 days?**	**Mon 1/3/05**	**Tue 2/1/05**
MAP WebSphere Application Server Rollout to Development & Production sites	**22 days?**	**Mon 1/3/05**	**Tue 2/1/05**
Acquire and read Redbook SG247072 "Planning for the installation and rollout of WSAM"	2 days	Mon 1/24/05	Tue 1/25/05
Build WSAM Location Specific Rollout Plan	**5 days?**	**Wed 1/26/05**	**Tue 2/1/05**
List of WebSphere (JVMs) to be monitored by WSAM	5 days	Wed 1/26/05	Tue 2/1/05
Define Application/owner to be deployed on WebSphere	1 day?	Wed 1/26/05	Wed 1/26/05
Complete rollout matrix (systems, time frames)	5 days	Wed 1/26/05	Tue 2/1/05
Define Monitoring Requirements (Who, WSAM, Traps)	1 day?	Wed 1/26/05	Wed 1/26/05
Identify Environment monitoring tools (Tec?) and plan WSAM trap integration	1 day?	Wed 1/26/05	Wed 1/26/05
ID Application transaction sizing (short term, long term)"	1 day?	Wed 1/26/05	Wed 1/26/05
Define Application Transaction Load (short/long term)	1 day?	Wed 1/26/05	Wed 1/26/05
Network Impact Planning	**1 day?**	**Mon 1/3/05**	**Mon 1/3/05**
Define Network Impact/Sizing	1 day?	Mon 1/3/05	Mon 1/3/05
Network Usage --> Network Engineering/Distribution Centers	1 day?	Mon 1/3/05	Mon 1/3/05
Network Usage --> Network Engineering/Home Office	1 day?	Mon 1/3/05	Mon 1/3/05
Define new load impact on WSAM Managing Server (System & Data Base)	1 day?	Mon 1/3/05	Mon 1/3/05
Production Server	1 day?	Mon 1/3/05	Mon 1/3/05

Figure D-1 WSAM sample installation project plan (Part 1 of 4)

Task Name	Duration	Start	Finish
Build Managing Server --> Application structure	**1 day?**	**Mon 1/3/05**	**Mon 1/3/05**
Define Monitoring Goal/Strategy by geography	1 day?	Mon 1/3/05	Mon 1/3/05
Define Monitoring strategy by work/application environment	1 day?	Mon 1/3/05	Mon 1/3/05
Consider DC & MS update process when definiing Connectivity Pools	1 day?	Mon 1/3/05	Mon 1/3/05
Define Network requirements for Managing Server	1 day?	Mon 1/3/05	Mon 1/3/05
Identify network/bandwith avaiability	1 day?	Mon 1/3/05	Mon 1/3/05
Size Managing Server Hardware requirements	1 day?	Mon 1/3/05	Mon 1/3/05
Hardware acquisition Plan for current/subsequent Managing Servers --> Budget process	1 day?	Mon 1/3/05	Mon 1/3/05
Complete local requirements for power, installation, network conectivity, database support	1 day?	Mon 1/3/05	Mon 1/3/05
WSAM MAINTENANCE	**1 day?**	**Mon 1/3/05**	**Mon 1/3/05**
Managing Server Maintenance (Production and Development)	1 day?	Mon 1/3/05	Mon 1/3/05
Define an update strategy for Production Location 1 to n	1 day?	Mon 1/3/05	Mon 1/3/05
Define an update strategy for Development Loction 1	1 day?	Mon 1/3/05	Mon 1/3/05
Data Base Maintenance	**1 day?**	**Mon 1/3/05**	**Mon 1/3/05**
Ongoing DB RUNSTAT, tuning, data trimming	1 day?	Mon 1/3/05	Mon 1/3/05
Database Backup	1 day?	Mon 1/3/05	Mon 1/3/05

Figure D-2 WSAM sample installation project plan (Part 2 of 4)

Task Name	Duration	Start	Finish
- Build HA PRODUCTION WSAM MANAGING SERVER	**38 days?**	**Mon 1/3/05**	**Wed 2/23/05**
Order Boxes (4)	38 days?	Mon 1/3/05	Wed 2/23/05
Move to Raised Floor <Fiber, Power, AC>	17 days?	Mon 1/3/05	Tue 1/25/05
Install Operating System (AIX)	10 days?	Mon 1/3/05	Fri 1/14/05
Install DB2 on Boxe 3 & 4 for WebSphere & failover testing- db2 license	6 days?	Mon 1/3/05	Mon 1/10/05
Populate WSAM data base	1 day?	Mon 1/3/05	Mon 1/3/05
Install WebSphere on Boxes 1 & 2	3 days?	Mon 1/3/05	Wed 1/5/05
Install WSAM Managing Server on Box 1 & 2	3 days?	Mon 1/3/05	Wed 1/5/05
Migrate one WebSphere Data Collector to the new Managing Server for testing.	1 day?	Mon 1/3/05	Mon 1/3/05
Installation Verification Test	2 days?	Mon 1/3/05	Tue 1/4/05
Migrate Applications to HA Box	14 days?	Mon 1/3/05	Thu 1/20/05
SAN Update to provide additional space	14 days?	Mon 1/3/05	Thu 1/20/05
Identify with DBA the maintenance to be performed	1 day?	Mon 1/3/05	Mon 1/3/05

Figure D-3 WSAM sample installation project plan (Part 3 of 4)

Task Name	Duration	Start	Finish
- Installation of WSAM onto Development Appliction Servers	**1 day?**	**Mon 1/3/05**	**Mon 1/3/05**
Install initial Data Collector onto first application server	1 day?	Mon 1/3/05	Mon 1/3/05
Test and verify installation	1 day?	Mon 1/3/05	Mon 1/3/05
Install Data Collectors onto subsequent like-type servers.	1 day?	Mon 1/3/05	Mon 1/3/05
Test and verify installation	1 day?	Mon 1/3/05	Mon 1/3/05
- Installation of WSAM onto Produciton Appliction Servers	**1 day?**	**Mon 1/3/05**	**Mon 1/3/05**
Install initial Data Collector onto first application server	1 day?	Mon 1/3/05	Mon 1/3/05
Test and verify installation	1 day?	Mon 1/3/05	Mon 1/3/05
Install Data Collectors onto subsequent like-type servers.	1 day?	Mon 1/3/05	Mon 1/3/05
Test and verify installation	1 day?	Mon 1/3/05	Mon 1/3/05
	1 day?	Mon 1/3/05	Mon 1/3/05
- TRAINING	**5 days?**	**Mon 1/3/05**	**Fri 1/7/05**
Set Training Timeline (Initial, Advanced)	1 day?	Mon 1/3/05	Mon 1/3/05
Define Training groups (operations, system, developers, capacity planners)	1 day?	Mon 1/3/05	Mon 1/3/05
Provide Training Class(es)	5 days	Mon 1/3/05	Fri 1/7/05
- INCORPORATE INTO EXISTING PRODUCTION MONITORING	**1 day?**	**Mon 1/3/05**	**Mon 1/3/05**
- TEC / NETCOOL Integration	**1 day?**	**Mon 1/3/05**	**Mon 1/3/05**
Acquire TEC/Netcools Specifications	1 day?	Mon 1/3/05	Mon 1/3/05
Define z/OS Monitoring Goals	1 day?	Mon 1/3/05	Mon 1/3/05
Define Distributed Monitoring Goals	1 day?	Mon 1/3/05	Mon 1/3/05
Define Test SNMP Traps	1 day?	Mon 1/3/05	Mon 1/3/05
Test TEC/Netcool integration	1 day?	Mon 1/3/05	Mon 1/3/05

Figure D-4 WSAM sample installation project plan (Part 4 of 4)

Related publications

The publications listed in this section are considered particularly suitable for a more detailed discussion of the topics covered in this IBM Redbook.

IBM Redbooks

For information on ordering these publications, see "How to get IBM Redbooks" on page 114. Note that some of the documents referenced here may be available in softcopy only.

- *Overview of WebSphere Studio Application Monitor and Workload Simulator,* SG24-6073
- *Installing WebSphere Studio Application Monitor V3.1*, SG24-6491

Other publications

These publications are also relevant as further information sources:

- *WebSphere Studio Application Monitor Installation and Customization Guide*, SC31-6312
- *WebSphere Studio Application Monitor CICS Data Collector Product Guide*, SC31-6569
- *WebSphere Studio Application Monitor Operations Guide*, SC31-6313
- *WebSphere Studio Application Monitor Monitoring Console User's Guide*, SC31-6314
- *WebSphere Studio Application Monitor Messages and Codes*, SC31-6315

Online resources

These Web sites and URLs are also relevant as further information sources:

- IBM WebSphere Studio Application Monitor Web page:

  `http://www-306.ibm.com/software/awdtools/studioapplicationmonitor/`
- The latest WebSphere Studio Application Monitor documentation:

  `http://www.ibm.com/software/awdtools/studioapplicationmonitor/library/`
- IBM z/OS Operating Systems Web page

  `http://www-1.ibm.com/servers/eserver/zseries/zos/`
- IBM WebSphere Product Family Web page: Description3

  `http://www-306.ibm.com/software/websphere/`
- IBM CICS Product Family Web page:

  `http://www-306.ibm.com/software/htp/cics/`
- IBM IMS Product Family Web page:

  `http://www-306.ibm.com/software/data/ims/`
- WebSphere MQ Product Family Web page:

  `http://www-306.ibm.com/software/integration/mqfamily/`

© Copyright IBM Corp. 2005. All rights reserved.

- IBM MVS Unix System Services (USS) Web page:

  http://www-1.ibm.com/servers/eserver/zseries/zos/unix/
- IBM Linux on zSeries® Web page:

  http://www-1.ibm.com/servers/eserver/zseries/os/linux/websp.html
- IBM Links to Java on z/OS Web pages:

  http://www-1.ibm.com/servers/eserver/zseries/software/java/related.html
- IBM DeveloperWorks Java Web pages:

  http://www-130.ibm.com/developerworks/java/
- IBM CICS Transaction Gateway Web page:

  http://www-306.ibm.com/software/htp/cics/ctg/overview.html
- IBM IMS Connect for z/OS Web page:

  http://www-306.ibm.com/software/data/db2imstools/imstools/imsconnect.html
- IBM AIX 5L Web page:

  http://www-1.ibm.com/servers/aix/
- Sun Solaris Operating System Web page:

  http://wwws.sun.com/software/solaris/
- Red Hat Linux Web page:

  http://www.redhat.com/
- Novell SUSE Linux Web page:

  http://www.novell.com/linux/suse/

How to get IBM Redbooks

You can search for, view, or download IBM Redbooks, Redpapers, Hints and Tips, draft publications, and Additional materials, as well as order hardcopy IBM Redbooks or CD-ROMs, at this Web site:

http://www.ibm.com/redbooks

Help from IBM

IBM Support and downloads:

http://www.ibm.com/support

IBM Global Services:

http://www.ibm.com/services

Index

© Copyright IBM Corp. 2005. All rights reserved.